MAGNA

a memoir of the enduring
human spirit

Also by Anderson Reynolds

They Called Him Brother George: Portrait of a Caribbean Politician (2023)

No Man's Land: A Political Introspection of St. Lucia (2021)

My Father Is No Longer There (memoir, 2019)

The Stall Keeper (novel, 2017)

The Struggle for Survival: an historical, political, and socioeconomic perspective of St. Lucia (creative non-fiction, 2003)

Death by Fire (novel, 2001)

MAGNA

a memoir of the enduring human spirit

ANDERSON REYNOLDS

JAKO BOOKS

Vieux Fort, New York, London

Published in the United States by Jako Books, a division of Jako Productions.

First Jako Books Edition, May 2025

www.jakoproductions.com

Copyright © 2025 by Anderson Reynolds

All rights reserved under International and Pan American Copyright Conventions. No part of this publication may be reproduced, stored in or introduced into a retrieval system, or transmitted, in any form or by any means (electronic, mechanical, photocopying, recording, or otherwise), without prior written permission of the publisher of this book.

Library of Congress Control Number (LCCN): 2025930426

ISBN-13:
978-1-963630-04-6

For my Brothers
and Sisters

Special thanks to Anya Achtenberg, Allan Weekes, Modeste Downes, Dr. Prosper Raynold, and Dr. Jolien Harmsen for their invaluable comments, suggestions, and encouragement, from which *Magna* benefited greatly.

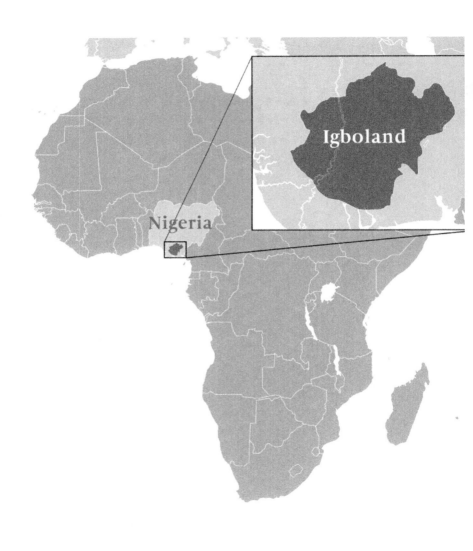

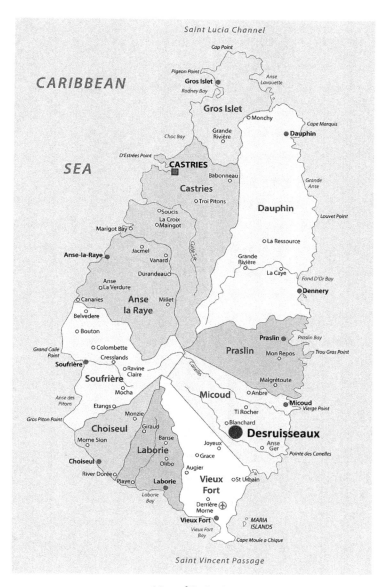

Map of St. Lucia

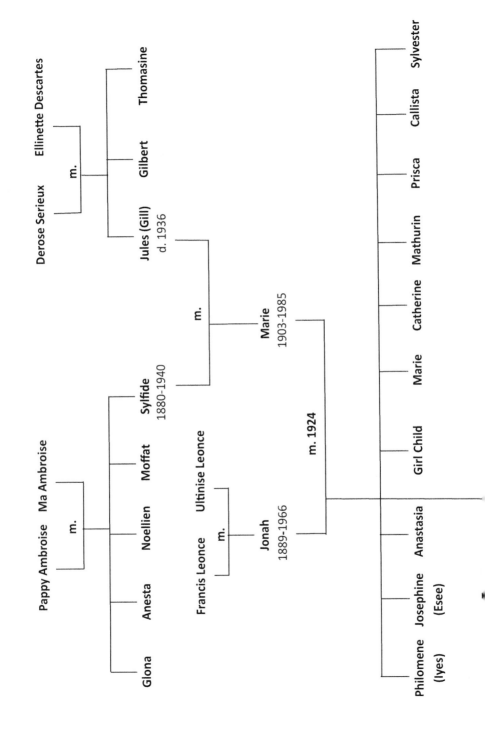

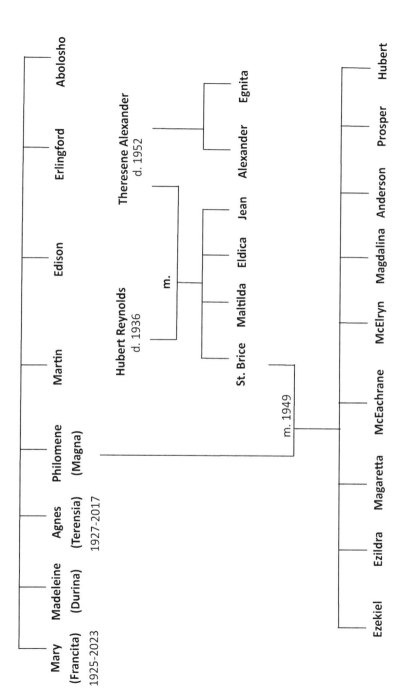

CONTENTS

Map of St. Lucia

Family tree

CHAPTER ONE *As My Mother Lay Dying* — 3

CHAPTER TWO *A Star Is Born* — 7

CHAPTER THREE *As My Mother Lay Dying* — 13

CHAPTER FOUR *Ancestors* — 26

CHAPTER FIVE *Desruisseaux* — 49

CHAPTER SIX *Saving the Day* — 57

CHAPTER SEVEN *The Moral of the Story* — 82

CHAPTER EIGHT *The Making of a Matriarch* — 105

CHAPTER NINE *Race, God and Politics* — 128

CHAPTER TEN *Wars and Pestilence* — 139

CHAPTER ELEVEN *Revolutions and Wedding Bells* — 151

CHAPTER TWELVE *London Calling* — 175

CHAPTER THIRTEEN *As My Mother Lay Dying* — 196

CHAPTER FOURTEEN *The Story of My Life* — 205

CHAPTER FIFTEEN *How to Live a Healthy and Productive Life in Old Age* — 221

CHAPTER SIXTEEN *As My Mother Lay Dying* — 240

CHAPTER SEVENTEEN *Thou Shalt Surely Die* — 245

CHAPTER EIGHTEEN *A Lesson on How Best to Die* — 250

CHAPTER NINETEEN *The Eulogy* — 255

Glossary — 262

Notes & References — 265

CHAPTER ONE

As My Mother Lay Dying

IT'S JUNE 2019. My mother Philomene, also known as Magna, also known as Ma Sido, is lying on her back on an air mattress set up on a hospital bed in the bedroom once shared with her husband of 52 years. He's been gone almost 20 years, mowed down by an out-of-control vehicle while on his early morning walk, just a few hundred yards down the road from the family home where his wife now lies.

My mother can move her arms and legs. She exercises them daily, lifting her arms and legs five to ten times. She has always believed in exercise. Besides working in her garden, she rode a stationary bike every morning. Not anymore. She can turn her head sideways but can't roll onto her side unaided, much less onto her front. Neither has she any desire to do so. Among other health conditions, she is suffering from vertigo, which I imagine creates the sensation when being moved that *she is falling, falling, falling down a precipice to her death.*

I don't think she remembers when and how she became ill. She probably has no sense of the ailment responsible for her predicament. But she knows she can't walk, that her legs won't support her. It's as if one day she just

Magna a memoir of the enduring human spirit

found herself in diapers and a hospital gown, on her back on a strange bed but in her own bedroom, unable to move around, unable to stand, unable to put on her sleeping gown, unable or unwilling even to feed herself.

Her bed is aligned with a window facing south toward the Caribbean Sea a few miles away. Outside this window, plum, soursop, and moringa trees are competing for sunlight. When tired of this scenery, she can turn her head left to the other window, facing east toward the Atlantic Ocean, also a few miles away. A cashew nut tree is brushing against this side of the house. With windows on two sides of the bedroom, the room is well-ventilated. A gentle breeze is forever present, offsetting the warm tropical weather. She insists the tree brushing against the house is a mango tree full of ripe mangoes for the taking and so urges her daughter, her devoted caregiver, to get her some.

"Zel, you eh see the tree full of mangoes? How come you all letting all the mangoes spoil? Zel, I have a taste for mangoes; go get me some; I will eat it with my breakfast."

"Mama, that's not mangoes. That's cashew."

"Zel, don't take me for a *papicho*. I'm telling you the mango tree full of ripe mangoes, birds there eating them, and you telling me nonsense. Zel, don't argue, just go get the mangoes."

Ezildra, whom family and friends call Zel, is my mother's eldest daughter and second child. She is a retired nurse and my mother's primary caregiver. My mother is as helpless as a newborn, so my sister has to do everything for her, including sponging, bathing, changing her diapers, brushing her teeth, putting on a fresh gown every morning, powdering her, combing her hair, dressing her bedsores, administering her medication, arranging doctor and lab appointments, holding the water bottle for her to drink through a straw, cooking, and spoon feeding her morning, noon and late afternoon.

But the way my mother bosses my sister around would make you think my mother is the nurse, the caregiver, the one in charge, and not the other way around. But Zel is used to that and doesn't seem to mind. She is of slight build. My mother, her patient, looks twice her size, a ship beside a lifeboat, which makes maneuvering her when providing care more challenging. Sometimes the thought occurs to me that Zel is being swallowed up by my mother, as if my mother is getting larger while Zel is getting smaller.

Zel is waging a battle on many fronts, and I'm afraid that caring for my mother is taking a toll on her health. Yet it's a bit comical watching my slightly built sister attempting to shift my large-bodied mother into desired positions, having to put her full body strength into the act. Of course, that's where I usually come in, helping to shift and hold my mother in required positions.

Despite my mother's helplessness, she hasn't lost her appetite and wants her meals on time, like clockwork. She hasn't lost her tongue either and thinks she is still in charge. But to my sister's credit, she is very accommodating. As if in keeping with her slight build, she is humble, soft-spoken, and shies away from the limelight. She has little appetite for gossip and talking ill of others. She has no wish to be the boss, but she is dutiful, never shirks responsibilities, goes beyond the call of duty, and puts others' interests above hers. So in terms of temperament, if not in size, mother and daughter are a good match. My mother couldn't ask for a better caregiver or a more devoted, tolerant, conscientious daughter.

Besides, they are each other's best friend and closest neighbors. Their homes are side by side in the same yard. Before my mother fell sick, they took turns cooking for the two households.

CHAPTER TWO

A Star Is Born

MY MOTHER was born on the Caribbean island of St. Lucia, in the rural hamlet of Desruisseaux, Micoud, on Sunday 20 January 1929, thus according to the star sign she was an Aquarius, and according to the Chinese Zodiac she was a Dragon. That year the heavens celebrated her birth by dimming the sun with two solar eclipses and two lunar eclipses. I don't know how these signs and heavenly manifestations conditioned her life and helped fashion her personality, or what other constellations of forces came together to give rise to her. But she was born in an auspicious year. In that year, as if mindful of her birth, the Privy Council, a British high court, decreed that Canadian women were persons and, therefore, eligible to be members of the legislature. Of course, my mother wouldn't have hesitated to tell them she needed no piece of paper or government approval to know she was a person, no more than she needed someone else's confirmation to know she was a woman and a mother.

That year St. Lucia witnessed the establishment of the Child Welfare Association and greeted the first airplane bringing mail to its shores. It was also the year of the great

Wall Street crash that heralded the Great Depression (1929 to 1941), the decade-long, worldwide economic depression that ravaged the world. So in the first year of my mother's life, blows were struck for women and children, and in the first decade of her life, the world was in the grip of an economic calamity.

As my mother lay dying at the ripe old age of 91 going on to 92, she repeated aloud, sometimes several times a day, the names of her nine children in the order of their birth—"Ezekiel, Ezildra, Magaretta, McEachrane, McElryn, Magdalina, Anderson, Prosper, Hubert."

I don't know why she did that. Whether it was to kill the boredom of lying there, nothing to do, nothing can do; or to relish, luxuriate in the existence of her children; or to exercise her memory muscles, thus keeping Alzheimer's, senility, at bay; or to make sure that in losing touch with the world, she never lost touch with her children. But what was clear to me was that we, her children, were her most precious things.

When my mother came into the world, she was greeted by three older siblings, all girls—Mary also known as Francita, Magdalene also known as Durina, and Agnes also known as Terensia. I suspect that after a string of three girls, my grandparents, my grandfather especially, were probably hoping and praying that this fourth child, my mother, would be a boy, which was understandable since in an era where subsistence farming was the primary source of livelihood and survival, boys came at a premium. If so, I'm not sure how joyful my grandparents were to receive my mother, and I'm not aware that any wise men or women attended her birth bearing gifts. I'm not even sure that as she took her first unaided breath and let go of her first wail, announcing to the world she had arrived, there was any sign, any birthmark, anything about her that signaled she would be the matriarch of the Francis clan, the one-of-a-kind woman she would become.

I know she was the fourth child of her parents, Jonah Francis and Marie Derose-Francis, whom we, their grandchildren, called Pa Jonah or Papa Jonah, and Ma Jonah or Mama Jonah or Ma J. I'm told that the next four of my mother's siblings, all boys, named Martin, Edison, Arlington, and Abolosho, died in childhood. We don't know what caused this string of deaths, whether it was the deprivation of the Great Depression years, or my mother was such a large and dominant presence that she precluded the survival of newcomers, boys especially. Or this was just the universe's way of punishing my grandparents for not welcoming my mother, not marking the occasion of her birth with sufficient gratitude and joy. Or they just didn't have much luck with boys. Or perhaps, in keeping with the island's superstitious beliefs, someone had placed obeah on the family to cut short the lives of the boys so my grandfather wouldn't have sons to help him support his family. I'm told that toward the end of the string of boys dying in childhood, my grandparents started giving the boys strange names, hence the name Abolosho, to confuse whatever evil people may have sent to do the boys harm.

Nonetheless, after the deaths of her brothers, my mother welcomed a succession of sisters into the family—Philomene also known as Iyes (who strangely was given the same name as my mother), Josephine also known as Essie, Anastasia also known as Bertha, and her seventh sister who sadly died as an infant. Next came Marie also known as Lily, and Catherine also known as Ulet. Then, as if by divine intervention or a lifting of the obeah curse, she greeted her brother Mathurin also known as Umen, the tenth child of the family who would survive childhood.

After Umen, she welcomed two more sisters into the family: Prisca and Callista also known as Tresa. Then she welcomed another miracle, Sylvester, also known as Mano, her second brother who would survive childhood. So she had twelve siblings—ten sisters and two brothers —who survived childhood. That is, children by Papa Jonah and Mama Jonah, for it turned out Papa Jonah had wandering eyes. He fathered at least two children out of wedlock—Rachel and Mathew—bringing the total number of my mother's known siblings to fourteen.

When my mother fell sick, never to get back on her feet, she spent a total of about ten weeks at a hospital five-minutes drive from her home in Vieux Fort, but when she was born, there was probably only one hospital in St. Lucia, which would have been in the capital city of Castries, about thirty miles away from Desruisseaux. This meant that as her mother's labor was coming on, there was no hospital readily accessible to take her to, nor were there qualified nurses or doctors to come to her assistance. She had to rely on a *fanmchay* (native midwife) with knowledge of bush medicine, most likely illiterate but heroic and legendary in those times, who learned her craft, not from any medical institution or as an apprentice to a trained doctor or nurse, but from folk wisdom and knowledge probably stretching back to Africa and passed on from one generation of *fanmchays* to the next.

A Star Is Born

The *fanmchay* would have had to rely on candles or kerosine lamps to guide her hand in helping Mama Jonah give birth (I don't know why, but somehow I have the vague notion that my mother made her grand entrance into the world in the middle of the night, not that there was anything inconspicuous about her) because there was not yet any electricity in most of the island's coastal towns and villages much less in the inland, rural hamlet of Desruisseaux, about four miles away from Micoud the closest town or village and about seven miles away from Vieux Fort the second closest town or village. The water to assist with the birth would have had to be heated on a coal pot because stoves (kerosine, gas, or otherwise) were unheard of in those parts. And the water for boiling would have been scooped from a large, waist-high clay jar sitting on the floor, the water collected and carried in calabash gourds from a spring steeply downhill from the house, for pipe-borne water in Desruisseaux was decades away.

The *tizan* the *fanmchay* would have given Mama Jonah to perk her up and ease the passage of the afterbirth would not have been any drug concocted in a lab and sold in a pharmacy but the *fanmchay's* own brew of sour orange, *shadobéni, makata, toussaint,* hog plum, *bois tasse, pieds poule, boné cawé, la vonique,* and *du thé pays.* Likewise, the *lok* the *fanmchay* would have prescribed for Mama Jonah to start taking several days after the birth for a duration of up to nine days would have been her own concoction of rum, castor oil, coconut oil, sour orange, bitter lemon, egg white, port wine, and maize water.

It was customary soon after birth to bury the *lonbwi* (umbilical cord, navel cord) under a golden apple tree or coconut tree that thereafter would belong to the child, or to place the *lonbwi* in a matchbox for safekeeping and given to the child at three years old to do the burying. I'm not sure which scenario applied to my mother and whether she remembered or was ever told under which tree her inheritance was buried. This practice was supposed to make the child prosperous and rooted in the land. I wonder whether it worked for my mother, and what were the full consequences of this act on her life.

The custom of burying the *lonbwi* under an economic tree was probably a carryover from Africa. For example, the Igbos, who, according to DNA tests, were likely my mother's African ancestors, followed the practice of mothers burying the naval cord of their newly born at the foot of an oil palm tree, local pear tree, breadfruit tree, local apple tree, or a plantain or banana plant. The appointed tree would thereafter be anointed the child's natal or naval plant and his inalienable inheritance. The Igbos believed that the plant's bountifulness would mirror the child's achievements as an adult. However, it seems the practice has more profound meaning and implications. The custom is thought to serve as a ritual dedicating the child early in life to the gods, the ancestors, and the community, as well as an introduction to the customs of the land, the customs of her people. It is said that an Igbo child whose naval cord wasn't buried cannot be a citizen, and one who doesn't know where her naval cord is buried is not a *diala*, not a freeborn or son of the soil.

CHAPTER THREE

As My Mother Lay Dying

MY MOTHER MAY NOT REMEMBER how it came to pass that she is on her back, unable to shift onto her side, much less sit up unaided, much less get off the bed and stand on her own two feet, much less take a walk to her veranda. But Monday 23 January 2017, when she first fell sick, is forever etched on my memory.

The day began as a sunny, nondescript tropical day, another typical day of my mother's golden years. She was up by her usual wakeup time of 5:30 AM, had studied her Bible lesson for the day, and prayed to her God, probably thanking Him for his benedictions, forbearance, guidance, and protection. Around 6:30, as she left her bedroom and stepped out onto her veranda to greet the new day, she was no doubt already anticipating the things she needed to do in her garden for the day —plant a row or two of cucumber, weed the patch of carrots, harvest some lettuce. Her neighborhood of upper St. Jude's Highway was already coming alive—the morning sun's rays were beginning to pierce the clouds, dogs were barking, roosters were still announcing the break of dawn, the din of traffic on the highway was picking up as commuters made their way to Vieux Fort and

Magna a memoir of the enduring human spirit

Castries to school, work, shopping, and vending. Some passersby were in not-so-quiet conversations, hummingbirds and ground doves were chirping in the fruit trees, a weed eater unmindful of late sleepers was getting a head start.

But then my mother screamed, "Zel!"

My sister was in the yard sweeping. I was in the kitchen getting coffee started in preparation for spending yet another day at my computer. We both rushed to the veranda, arriving there at the same time. "Mama, what happened? You, okay?"

Our mother was anything but okay. She was down on her buttocks on the cold, tiled veranda floor. She was shivering. Her voice was barely audible. She was making an effort, but only mumbled sounds came out. My sister touched her back and chest and said she had a high fever. We helped her up, but her legs denied her support. We sat her down. Taking no chances, we immediately helped her to my car and took her to the hospital about five minutes away.

At this point, it was no longer an ordinary business-as-usual day. The world had changed. My world had changed, my sister's world had changed, and most of all, my mother's world had changed.

Hearing my mother's scream, then seeing her helpless on the floor, unable to stand on her feet, and she who was never at a loss for words suddenly losing her voice, a flutter passed through my head. I grew weak, my body froze. I could barely speak; speaking coherently took every ounce of my willpower and mental resolve. My feet suddenly felt too feeble, too weak to support me; it felt like one step and I would fall.

I didn't know it then, but over the next few years, this sensation would come over me each time my mother suffered a setback and we had to call the ambulance to take her to the hospital.

No sooner than we arrived at the hospital, my mother was wheeled to the emergency room. Several patients were there on beds in spaces separated by curtains. After a brief update from my sister, the hospital staff took a reading of my mother's blood pressure and blood sugar and her other vital signs. They confirmed my mother's high fever. They took blood and urine samples to perform urinalysis, complete blood count, renal function test, troponin test, creatine kinase, and creatine kinase-MB. The urine sample was collected without much difficulty, but the blood sample was a different story. The nurse couldn't find a vein in my mother's arm for drawing blood. She made so many attempts that I feared my mother's arm would resemble that of a needle junkie. Finally, she tried her leg and met with success.

It was well past noon when my mother was moved to a medical ward, which she would share with seven to ten other patients and which, to our great chagrin, would remain her home for seven weeks. The only privacy afforded her and her ward mates was drawing curtains to surround their beds when the nurses cared for their personal needs. It seems the hospital was short-staffed. Besides administering the usual care, the nurses were the ones who had to bathe the patients. Once, I helped a nurse turn over a heavy-set, elderly patient who had her diaper changed. Sadly, during my mother's stay, several patients, some arriving after her, died on the ward. With each passing day, I became increasingly apprehensive that this would be my mother's fate.

The readings and lab results indicated my mother was diabetic and hypertensive and had a low red blood count. No news there; we already knew that, and between my sister and my mother's family doctor, her blood pressure and blood sugar levels were being monitored and managed. Besides hypertension and diabetes, she had been suffering from vertigo and a nerve condition.

The test results brought the doctors no closer to a diagnosis of my mother's illness. Weeks passed, but they had no diagnosis to share. Instead, we were under the distinct impression that they were avoiding us. On some days, in the hope of talking to a doctor for an update on my mother's illness, we waited in vain at the hospital for almost half a day. Rarely were we able to meet with a doctor, much less get one to apprise us of our mother's prognosis and care plan.

Meanwhile, at night my mother was screaming and calling out the names of her children, disturbing the sleep of the other patients. During the day, she was bossing the nurses around, giving them a hard time, saying, in effect, her body may be impaired, may have failed her, but not her mind, and definitely not her tongue.

Her condition got much worse before it got better. In the third week of her stay in the hospital, she stopped passing stool. The head of the medical department called an urgent family meeting. With great earnestness, he told us our mother didn't have bowel movements and an operation was needed right away to rectify the problem. Without the operation, she would not last long. We knew that to operate on an eighty-seven-year-old with multiple morbidities was courting disaster. But what choice did we have? Here was the head of the medical department, the ultimate authority on the subject, telling us that if they didn't operate right away, our mother would surely die. We resigned ourselves to the situation and with great misgivings agreed to the operation. This was around 9 AM, but around 4 PM, we got another urgent call to meet with the head of the medical department. This time around, he informed us that after consulting with the surgical team, they had decided to administer an oral laxative, and that had done the trick; my mother's bowel movement was back on track.

I thought, *what kind of thing is this? Is he a quack, or what? You mean to tell me he didn't consult with the surgical team before bulldozing us into agreeing to go along with the operation, but once he brought it to their attention, realizing that if the operation went awry, they would be the ones culpable, the surgical team took the extra step, the extra precaution, of trying a less risky, less invasive approach, and lo and behold it worked. Operations, thanks, but no thanks!*

This brought to mind some of the negative things people were saying about St. Jude Hospital. That patients were dying needlessly because, often, they were misdiagnosed and administered the wrong treatment and medication.

However, one can hardly blame the hospital staff, the nurses especially, for this sad state of affairs. On the contrary, one needed to be sympathetic. In 2009, a fire gutted St. Jude Hospital, forcing authorities to relocate it to the George Odlum National Sports Stadium, which was to serve merely as a makeshift disaster relief medical facility.

But ten years later, after over US$74 million had been spent on rebuilding the hospital, it was nowhere near completion. The politicians had turned the rebuilding effort into a blame game, a political football, and some would say a vehicle of corruption and economic extraction.[1] So for all practical purposes, the stadium had become a permanent hospital. Yet besides being ill-suited to that purpose, it had fallen into disrepair: its roof rained fiberglass particles, exposure to which was causing adverse health reactions among hospital staff, forcing some to go on sick leave. An official inspection by an independent occupational safety and health specialist revealed that the makeshift hospital was grossly deficient, inhospitable, and an occupational safety and health hazard.[2] One doctor summarized the conditions as a "dungeon of shame."

In addition to these reports and the absence of a diagnosis of my mother's ailment, the conduct of the medical department head did nothing but deepen my apprehension about the quality and appropriateness of the care my mother was receiving. We never met with him again; we saw him only from a distance, hurrying along as if on a life-and-death mission.

Our fears were confirmed a week later when my mother took a turn for the worse. She stopped eating, lost her speech, and showed no signs of recognizing any of us. She lay there inert, lifeless, as if in a coma. The Saturday of that week, in the late afternoon, we—myself, my eldest brother and his wife, my eldest sister, my youngest sister and her oldest son—gathered at my mother's hospital bed. She was oblivious to our presence. We were all in tears or holding back tears. As one, we thought she wouldn't last another

As My Mother Lay Dying

day, and this was the last time we would see her alive; this was likely our last goodbye.

Thankfully, she survived the weekend of our despair, and by Monday the hospital informed us that they had diagnosed her illness. She had contracted pneumonia. Now, with a diagnosis, the hospital was able to administer the appropriate medication, and my mother miraculously returned to the world of the living. She regained her focus and appetite, and her tongue was again active. I thought, *so it wasn't the sickness that had reduced my mother to a coma; it had been the wrong medication she was taking.* I rejoiced at my mother's recovery but became even more wary of the care on offer at St. Jude Hospital.

My mother was discharged in the second week of March 2017. She was still relatively weak; she couldn't walk, she would never walk again. An ambulance took her home. From then on, all her visits to the hospital would be by ambulance.

Thanks to the hospital stay, bedsores had colonized my mother's buttocks. She complained of pain and discomfort. She screamed, cried, and cursed when she was being shifted onto her side for bed baths and treatment of her bedsores. She slept day and night as if in hibernation, barely waking for meals, treatment, and medication. However, gradually, under my sister's 24-hour loving care (she took to sleeping in my mother's bedroom on an extra bed), her condition improved. The bedsores were healing, her complaints of pain and discomfort grew less and less, she stayed awake longer, and displayed a greater appetite for conversation.

About the fourth month after her hospital discharge, we decided it was time to occasionally get her off the bed and out on the veranda to begin the process of her mental and physical rehabilitation. Up till then, it hadn't occurred to us that she would never walk again, never return to her old self, her life before taking ill. She would have none of our rehabilitation interventions. Her legs couldn't support her weight; they buckled under her, so we had to bodily lift her into the wheelchair. She cursed, screamed, and cried, "God, I'm dying; God, I'm dying." She resisted, refused to be lifted, refused to get on the wheelchair, holding on tight to the bed with a strength and tenacity we didn't know she possessed. Apparently, because of her vertigo condition, the act of lifting her induced a bodily sensation of spinning and falling as if, I suspect, from a precipice. So in her mind, staying on the bed was a matter of life and death. We had little choice but to postpone the intervention.

We tried again the following week, and this time we were prepared. We refused to take no for an answer. Her life as she once knew it was at stake. We pried her hands from the bed and, against her screaming and tongue-lashing, lifted her bodily onto the wheelchair and wheeled her to the veranda. She paid no attention to her garden, to the outside world, but kept complaining of pain and discomfort and crying, begging us to take her back to bed. We returned her to bed after about 30 minutes.

Over time, as she gained strength, slept less, and became more alert, though she remained fearful of getting into the wheelchair, she resisted less, seemed to enjoy the outing, and was willing to stay out longer. By then we had come to accept the reality that she may never walk again, and her current situation was likely her new normal.

For her part, she behaved as if that's how she had come into the world; that's how she had always been and would have it no other way. We just had to serve her meals on time, provide whatever food or drink she had a taste for, plait her hair nicely, change her gown daily, and ensure that family, friends, neighbors, and her Adventist brothers and sisters kept up their visits.

However, she lost all interest in what was happening in the world outside her bedroom. She refused to watch television. We turned on the radio in the bedroom for her, but she didn't care one way or the other.

Most unbelievable and probably alarming was that the person who most of her life had been inseparable from her garden, spending the better part of each day lovingly tending it, hiring people to make the beds and construct aerial planting boxes, collecting rainwater in drums for watering her plants, consulting her Farmer's Almanac for when best to plant, lost all interest in what was once her handicraft, her masterpiece, now barely taking note of it. The most interest she displayed was to request that we pick jelly coconuts for her and, for no explicable reason, demanded that we cut down the two lime trees in the yard.

I would tell her, "Ma Sido, look at your garden; it needs some serious work."

She would reply, "So?"

Equally alarming was that this once independent, proactive, industrious woman who was always on her feet was now perfectly willing, would have it no other way, to be totally dependent on others. She provided no help when we put her in the wheelchair or shifted her sideways to administer care. She refused to feed herself even when she seemed quite capable. It was as if she were content to be a baby, as if my sister had just given birth to a bossy, complaining, oversized baby. As if after eighty-plus years of constant work, of living for and taking care of others, of having to be the one holding up the fort, putting out the fire, making the life and death decisions, she had decided to let go of her load, put her feet up, let others take care of her every need, be as dependent on others as some were once dependent on her. That it was time people returned the favor. That after eighty-plus years of hard and dedicated labor, she was bone tired. Too tired even to feed herself, take a walk, or take an interest in the garden crafted by her own hands. So in the manner of the song, *Study War No More*, she laid down all her burden by the bedside, laid down her sword and shield (but kept her tongue intact), and was no longer studying war, taking on the world.

I would tell her, "Mama, you there behaving like a baby. Do you think you're a baby? You're not a baby, you know. You eh lifting a finger to help yourself?"

She would either ignore me or say: "Anderson, *kité mwem bat mizè mwem*; Anderson, leave me alone." Or "Anderson, *mwen za sav ou pa kontan mwen;* Anderson, I already know you don't love me."

Of course, she knew she didn't have to pay me any mind because I didn't much matter. My sister was the one she needed, the one her whole existence depended on.

By THE SECOND YEAR OF MY MOTHER'S ILLNESS, we had arrived at a new normal, a plateau, if you will. My mother's

As My Mother Lay Dying

daily routine—her baths, backrubs, bedsore treatment, medications, meals, veranda visits, and the regular company of family, friends, and neighbors—was well established. The only break in that routine was when we had to take her to the hospital for checkups, x-rays, and lab tests, or when my sister thought something was amiss.

However, I hated the very idea of my mother going to the hospital. Each time, the same weakness I had experienced when she first fell ill would wash over me. Seeing her frightened, disoriented, not fully understanding what was going on, strapped by strangers to a stretcher, carried and loaded into an ambulance like a sack of yams onto a donkey cart, brought lab rats to mind. Each time, no matter what brought her to the hospital, she ended up spending almost half the day in the ER. Each time, she was subjected to the same barrage of tests.

My sister knew all this but didn't seem to mind the hospital at all. It seemed to me that at the least provocation, she was happy to call the ambulance and accompany our mother to this place that no less of an authority than a medical doctor called a "dungeon of shame." At first, I couldn't understand why, because, left to me, I would have taken her to the hospital only when absolutely necessary. This place was bad news to me. Under my sister's care, my mother's bedsores would be just about healed, but no sooner than we took her to the hospital and she was kept there for a few days for observation, the sores would return in full force, giving my sister the Herculean task of once again fighting to bring her back to health. It was only upon reflection, after putting myself in my sister's shoes, that I gained an appreciation, a better perspective of where she was coming from.

Here she was, bearing the full burden of caring for our mother, being responsible for whether she lives or dies. With such a heavy burden, my sister couldn't take any chances; she had to make sure of never being the cause of any health setbacks. One of my siblings seemed to agree with this explanation for my sister's cautiousness. He reasoned that primary caregivers like my sister are worried that their patients might die on their watch, and they may be blamed or blame themselves for not acting judiciously, which makes them inefficiently cautious.

Another reason my sister may have welcomed our mother's visit and stay at the hospital was that it afforded her a mental breather because she was able to share with or transfer to the hospital staff the responsibility for my mother's wellbeing. So no matter how brief my mother's hospital stay, my sister obtained a mental and physical breather, a vacation of sorts. Mind you, she had no complaints about taking care of my mother, spending time with her, which she welcomed, which was her greatest pleasure, which she wouldn't have had any other way; from that she didn't desire a break. After all, her patient wasn't just her mother. She was her best friend, her closest confidant.

Apart from my mother's stay at the hospital, the only real break my sister received was the weekends when my youngest sister came home to relieve her from her duties.

Caring for my mother calmed down even more when, instead of taking her to the hospital for check-ups and lab work, we contracted a doctor for regular home visits, and when required, a lab technician came to collect lab samples. With this approach, we rarely had reason to take her to the hospital.

Marie "Derose" Francis, Magna's mother and the
Eve of the Francis clan

CHAPTER FOUR

Ancestors

AS MY MOTHER LAY BEDRIDDEN, dead people visited her, or so she says. She sees them walking past her bedroom window, some greeting and talking to her. But she didn't share the subject matter of these conversations with us. My eldest brother and his wife believed my mother was on to something. They surmised that ghosts or the spirits of the dead are all around, but maybe only those like my mother, at the border of life and death, are privileged to see and converse with them.

I'm very skeptical of obeah, witchcraft, and all such supposed supernatural manifestations; I group them in the same category as the many conspiracy theories floating around. I am even skeptical of the existence of God and Satan, and the older I get the more skeptical I become. So I'm more tempted to believe that my mom, in her delirium, was seeing things that weren't there, and what she saw were, like dreams, merely the outcropping of her subconscious mind. Yet, I was still wondering whether her mind was taking her back to her maternal grandparents, Gill and Ma Gill, and her mother and father, Papa Jonah and Mama Jonah. And if my brother and his wife were correct that she could see ghosts, I wondered whether she was able to see and enter into fellowship with her ancestors back to even before she was born; those she never met, those, for example, who never left the shores of Africa.

Slave narratives revealed that enslaved persons in St. Lucia were subjected to a barrage of cruel punishments. However, of these brutalities, the barrel atrocity seems to stand out most in the collective memory of my grandmother's generation. The offending enslaved person was imprisoned in a barrel that once held rum for shipment to Europe, then lots of nails were pounded into the barrel, which was then rolled down a hill. I imagine that if my mother were privy to the ghosts of the distant past, the ghosts of her ancestors who met such ghastly deaths must have come screaming in anguish.

During the colonial era, there was constant warfare between France and England for St. Lucia. So much so that, as tourist brochures love to romanticize, the island changed hands no less than thirteen times between the two nations. It was said that during these battles, when British victory was imminent, the French planters buried their treasures to keep them out of the hands of the English, often beheading an enslaved person and burying the head with the treasure so that the spirit of the enslaved person would keep guard over it.

I wondered whether the ghost of the beheaded enslaved had alerted my mother to the whereabouts of any such buried treasure, which would not have been any more unusual than the case of her youngest sister, who, in her early twenties, had received one such cache of buried treasure in a dream. In the dream, she was told to bring along her nephew, whom Mama Jonah was raising, when she went for the treasure. However, she went with a family friend instead of her nephew. They found no signs of the treasure at the location specified in the dream. So, on my aunt's next attempt, she brought just her nephew, and this time they found a silver table fork marking the location of the buried treasure. For verification, while her nephew remained on guard at the spot, my aunt took the fork to show Mama Jonah. On her return, she once again brought along the friend. With great anticipation, all three—my aunt, her nephew, and the friend—dug for the treasure. But as they were digging, they heard a rumbling, earth-cracking sound of something descending into the bowels of the earth, and, for their efforts, all they found were broken pieces of the type of clay jar in which people have the habit of burying treasure. It seems that by bringing along the friend, a clear violation of the dream's instructions, my aunt had forfeited her gifted treasure.

I'm unsure of my mother's supernatural powers, but if she had been born 95 years earlier, before 1834, before emancipation, she would most likely have been born into slavery because most of the island's black population was enslaved. And if she had been born 122 years earlier, before 1807, the year the British abolished the slave trade, she would most likely have been captured and exported from Igboland, Nigeria, because DNA ancestry results suggest she was 89.3 % West African, 3.7% other African, and 5.9% European; and of her West African ancestry, she was 48.9% Igbo (Nigerian), 32.3% Ghanaian, Liberian and Sierra Leonean, and 8.1% other West African.

Ancestors

My mother may have been proud of her African heritage, but she would not have been amused that the Igbos, the people she most likely came from, were actively involved in the Atlantic slave trade, selling their fellow Africans to the Europeans as human cargo.

Interestingly, my own DNA ancestry results suggest that I was even more of an Igbo than my mother, for the DNA results indicate that I was 85.5 percent West African, and of this West African heritage, I was 61.7% Igbo compared to my mother's 48.9%.

As an enslaved person, it is unlikely my mother would have lived to the ripe old age of a month shy of 92 because the enslaved, more so those of the West Indies as opposed to those of the American South, had an aborted life expectancy. The evidence[3] suggests that enslaved West Indians faced even harsher conditions than those in the American South. The death rate of enslaved West Indians was one-third higher, and in the early 19th century enslaved women in the U.S. South gave birth to twice as many children as their West Indian counterparts. So while the enslaved in the American South were able to increase their numbers by natural reproduction, the population of enslaved West Indians could only be sustained by fresh imports. Consequently, the enslaved in the West Indies had a higher proportion of recent arrivals from Africa than those in the U.S. South, where, over time, the enslaved population became primarily American-born.

Given my mother's heroic and indomitable spirit, she would most likely have been one of the enslaved who took every opportunity to sabotage the slave plantation system. However, she would have zealously tended her garden plot to cultivate her independence, and like the famous St. Lucian *Neg Maron* or *gens libres* leader, Flore Bois Gaillard, who was a thorn in the side of the invading British army (that insisted on upholding bondage on the island after, following the French Revolution, France had decreed the abolition of slavery), she would have led slave revolts and join the *Neg Marons* in their escape from slavery to the hills and forests where they established their *gens libres* settlements.

In fact, there is evidence[4] to suggest that the Neg Marons operated in the Desruisseaux area. Archeologists have discovered the tunnels they built along the Canelles River near Desruisseaux that served as lookouts and hideaways. They also found *Neg Maron tou san fon* (bottomless holes) and caves in nearby Anse Ger.

It is said that some of the more adventurous and proactive enslaved persons portalled back to Africa by building bonfires on the beach and then jumping over the fire three times, and others by simply jumping over a basin of water. If there is any truth to that, I do not doubt that as an enslaved person my mother would have been among those who portalled back to Africa.

IF MY BROTHER AND HIS WIFE'S THEORY of ghosts holds any water, it is conceivable that Jules Derose (Gill), my mother's maternal grandfather, who was originally from the village of Micoud, had visited her as she lay bedridden with nothing but time on her hands. His mother, Elliette Descartes, was first married to Joseph Chrystophe, who died sometime between 1855 and 1860, leaving Elliette Descartes a widow, but not for long, because she then married Derose Serieux, and the union produced three offspring—Thomasin and the twin brothers, Gilbert and Jules.

My mother described her grandfather, Jules Derose, whom she referred to as Gill, as a short, slightly built man with a mulatto complexion and a quiet disposition. He must have inherited his mulatto complexion from his mother, Elliette Descartes, who was a descendant of Norbert Descartes, a Frenchman who owned hundreds of acres of land wedged between Volet and Fond Estates in the Micoud North area. Uncle Mano revealed that Nobert Descartes had a child with either his maid or his enslaved house servant, and that child is the progenitor of Elliette Descartes, and hence that of Gill, my mother's grandfather.

According to family folklore, Norbert Descartes had prepared a will stipulating that none of his property should be sold and that his estate must remain in the hands of his St. Lucian heirs. Of course, the problem is that given St. Lucia's family land tenure system (whereby entire families receive or inherit land undivided among individual members) and Descartes' heirs having multiplied to large numbers and scattered to all corners of the island and beyond, securing their inheritance would be a nightmarish undertaking.

Escap, an upscale housing development between Micoud and Mon Repos that overlooks the Atlantic Ocean, sits on land once part of the Descartes estate. As is customary, the government had gazetted the accumulated delinquent property taxes on the land, but when the notice period expired without any of the legal owners coming forward to pay the tax arrears, the government apparently sold the property to the Escap developers to recover the out-

Magna a memoir of the enduring human spirit

standing taxes. So ironically, in violation of the spirit of Descartes's will, his estate, or at least part of it, has fallen into the hands of strangers. Another irony is that one of my cousins has since bought land from the Escap developers, essentially buying what already belonged to her.

SYLFIDE, my mother's maternal grandmother, whom she called Ma Gill, was born and raised in Desruisseaux (around 1880), near where my mother grew up. Her parents, Pappy Ambroise and Ma Ambroise, had four other children—Glona, Anesta, Noellien, and Moffat. My mother intimated that it would be very difficult to find another husband and wife as different from one another as were her grandparents. Gill was of mulatto complexion and slight build; Ma Gill was stout, of dark complexion, and un-deniably African. Gill was quiet, gentle, and unobtrusive; Ma Gill was an overbearing woman who delighted in or-dering people around and getting them to do most of her chores. She had no problems sitting around while her hus-band did the cooking and other house chores.

My mother said that her mother, Marie Derose Francis (Ma Jonah), would often send one of her children to do chores and run errands for Ma Gill, sometimes making them spend the night with her. Some of her sisters balked at this custom, hated it, and would do their best to avoid being the sacrificial lamb. But not my mother. She didn't mind at all. She looked forward to spending time with her grandmother and doing her bidding. When Ma Gill had to journey to Vieux Fort, a seven-mile, two to three-hour trek from Desruisseaux, it was my mother she took along, os-tensibly to carry on her head a calabash gourd filled with

Ma Gill's drinking water because she wouldn't drink water from any and every source, it had to be from the spring on her homestead.

When my mother was sharing this story, I never asked why she was so willing to comply with the wishes of her grandmother, who it seemed to me was *abizan* (abusive). But then again, I think I already knew the answer. There wasn't one lazy bone in my mother's body. If nothing needed doing, she would find a way to create work, so it must have been my mother's great pleasure to be in a situation where there were always tasks to perform, keeping her in constant demand.

Gill and Ma Gill died four years apart. Gill was the first to depart—Sunday 29 March 1936—two months after my mother's seventh birthday. Ma Gill died on Monday 17 June 1940 from a cerebral hemorrhage; she was 60 years old. My mother was eleven and a half years old. So by the time my mother was a teenager, she was already without grandparents.

Ma Gill's passing was probably the first death to touch my mother profoundly and of which she was fully cognizant. As Ma Gill's only child, Mama Jonah would have been at the center of the burial and wake activities, so my mother would have had ample opportunity to follow the activities closely. Ma Gill hadn't favored Papa Jonah for her daughter, but ironically, as the head of his household, he was principally responsible for her funeral and burial. It was he who, no sooner had she been pronounced dead, came and measured the body and built her coffin. In those days, people had to be buried within two days of death. So the very day of Ma Gill's death, or no later than the following day, her body would have been washed (most likely with holy water) and dressed in her Sunday-best attire. The coffin would have been draped with either a black cashmere or a black cotton cloth (*koton nwè*), placed on two boards (*sevyé*), and carried to the church and cemetery by four men. Wakes were held the same night as the person's death. Children were not allowed to attend wakes, so I'm not sure how much of Ma Gill's wake my mother had witnessed. But if her wake was typical of those at the time, hers was an all-night affair of rum and strong coffee, of hymns, storytelling, jokes, drama, *kont,* and *Kutumba* accompanied by a folk band.

My mother told the story of a man who had succumbed to cholera during a mini outbreak of the dreadful disease. In the middle of crossing a river on their way to take the corpse to burial, the pallbearers heard a pounding sound coming from the coffin; in their shock and fright, they dropped their burden. When they caught themselves and opened the coffin, the dead man, like Christ rising from the grave, got out, stepped into the river, and walked. I can well imagine that with their belief in superstition, the people saw this as a miracle by either God or the Devil. But I imagined that, given the unscientific method at the time of ascertaining death and the necessity of burying the dead the same day of death or the day after for the latest, quite a few people got buried alive. Hopefully, Ma Gill wasn't one of them.

If my mom's mind wasn't playing tricks on her as she lay bedridden, and her grandparents, Gill and Ma Gill, indeed came visiting, I wondered what they said to her. I can well imagine them telling her how proud they were of her and all she had accomplished, and expressing pleasant surprise at how Marie, their one child, who became Ma Jonah, had given rise to a nation.

THE UNION of Jules Derose Serieux and Sylfide Ambroise (Gill and Ma Gill) produced only one child, Marie Derose, my grandmother, my mother's mother. She was born Sunday 7 June 1903 and baptized Sunday 12 July at the Micoud Roman Catholic Church, with her aunt Anesta Ambroise and a friend of the family, Jasmin Baptiste, serving as godparents.

It seems that Mama Jonah took after her father and was the opposite of her mother. She was calm, quiet, and soft-spoken. My mother said that as an only child, her mother was spoiled and sheltered, and even as an adult remained innocent or naive of the ways of the world. "*Un ti inosan*, a little innocent," my mother said. She said that when her father, Jonah Francis, was displeased with his wife, her mother, he would punish her with a whip just as he would any of his daughters, and apparently Mama Jonah was just as accepting of the punishment.

It seems Mama Jonah grew up with privileges. Her grandfather, Pappy Ambroise, owned over 20 acres of land, one-fifth of which had been inherited by her mother, Ma Gill. Her father, Gill, was heir to Micoud lands and had purchased several parcels in the Desruisseaux and Blanchard area. Moreover, in those days, separate from Gill's wealth, his mulatto complexion and somewhat "nice hair" (straight hair) would have given him additional standing in society.

When Mama Jonah was growing up, the importance of land as a means of survival and prestige could not be overstated. After all, one of the main things that separated the enslaved from their owners was land ownership. In those days, people literally lived off the land. They grew most of the food that landed on their plates. Farine and cassava bread, made from the cassava they cultivated, served as a substitute for cereal and bread. Moreover, it wasn't unusual for them to make flour out of banana, plantain, and *makabou*. The basic materials for building their homes—lumber, bamboo, shingles, palm leaves, clay mud—were all obtained from the land. So, too, were the materials for making baskets, rope, and kitchen utensils like bowls, spoons, drinking water containers, etc. Their mattresses and pillows were made out of cotton or coconut husk fiber. The animals that served as meat and means of transportation were raised and fed on the land. Consequently, with the barter system and cooperative work strategies such as *koudmen*, they could get by with a minimal amount of money, used mainly to purchase a few essentials such as cloth, tools, saltfish, sugar, and salt.

Land may have been crucial for the survival of the people, but owning it was no small feat for the descendants of formerly enslaved people. After emancipation, the planters were faced with the rude awakening that they could no longer access large pools of enslaved labor over which they had complete control and to which they only needed to pay token wages. So with the help of the colonial government, they took steps to deny the formerly enslaved access to land as a means of forcing them to remain latched to the plantations and be totally dependent on them for their existence. They threatened to evict the ex-slaves (or forced them to pay rent) from the huts and vegetable plots they had occupied during slavery if they were to refuse to work on the plantations when and as needed; they imposed licensing fees on horses and other means of transportation, as well as on hucksters and fishing boats; they set land prices artificially high and the minimum acreage size at which crown lands could be sold beyond the means of the formerly enslaved; they forced households to provide eight days per year of free road service labor; and they taxed the agricultural produce (such as ground provisions, charcoal, cocoa, and wood) commonly cultivated or produced by the formerly enslaved while exempting sugar, rum, and other sugarcane byproducts produced mainly by the plantocracy.

So the Gills' ownership of considerable fertile land was a definite sign that they were of some standing in Desruisseaux, and their daughter, my grandmother, had a privileged upbringing. Her privileged life was also evident in the fact that she had completed a primary school education and could read and write, even serving briefly as a teacher at a time when the majority of St. Lucians didn't attend school and remained illiterate, more so those living away from the coastal settlements in such interior rural hamlets as Desruisseaux.

I DON'T KNOW as much about Papa Jonah as I know about Mama Jonah. From the family, I understood that Papa Jonah was from Vieux Fort and an orphan, partly raised by the Roman Catholic priests at the Vieux Fort parish, where he served as an acolyte. Growing up, he was what people unflatteringly called a boat boy, a name given to boys who loitered at the fishermen's bay helping to pull the fishing pirogues, called *kannòt*, onto shore, haul fishing

Magna a memoir of the enduring human spirit

gear, and run errands for the fishermen. But when he met Mama Jonah, he was already a fisherman going to sea on a *kannòt vwèl* (pirogue with sails).

My mother's birth certificate listed Papa Jonah as a fisherman. While I heard about the parents of Mama Jonah, I heard or read nothing about those of Papa Jonah, except that his marriage certificate listed Francis Leonce and Ultinise Leonce as his legitimate parents. If so, I reckon his real surname was Leonce and not Francis. This faux pas of carelessly assigning a father's Christian name as his children's surname was common in St. Lucia.

Papa Jonah's uncle, whom we called *Tonton* Maise, Uncle Maise, was the only relative of Papa Jonah I knew growing up. My eldest brother said that *Tonton* Maise had spent much time in French Guiana and was a tall, strapping man. But I remember him as a tall, bent-double, almost bedridden older man for whom my mother prepared the meals we took to him in aluminum *carriers*. He must have been a joiner or carpenter by trade because his tiny, one-room, shingle-covered house was crowded with such tools and products of the trade as hammers, anvils, saws, toy carts, figurines, wood carvings, etc. I also remember he staged puppet shows with puppets made of wood. Uncle Mano said *Tonton* Maise was a true craftsman, a true artist; in addition to the beloved show puppets, he crafted all kinds of carvings and figurines.

How did the sheltered, privileged, shy damsel of Desruisseaux, Marie Derose, my grandmother, meet Jonah Francis, the Vieux Fort orphan and street-smart fisherman? According to Uncle Mano, they met in Vieux Fort at the fish depot, and it seems that it had been love at first sight for Papa Jonah. He was so smitten with the Desruisseaux damsel that when she came alongside his *kannòt* at the depot to buy fish, he forgot about all other customers, forgot that he was there to collect payment for his fish, even, and made sure she got all the fish she wanted, and more.

I can picture the petite, demure Desruisseaux maiden somehow managing against the odds to make her way to the front of the *kannòt*, through the sweaty, noisy surrounding crowd clamoring for fish, and as my grandfather in his wet, raggy fishing outfit, a pile of fish in front of him, looked up from the *kannòt*, his eyes fell into hers for the first time, changing his world forever. That's how I imagine the Desruisseaux damsel met the fisherman and how he began making an impression on her.

Around the time Marie Derose was making the acquaintance of her husband-to-be, her mother had found a match for her, a well-to-do friend of the family from Desruisseaux with a great deal of land. But apparently, Marie wasn't in the least bit interested. She found the would-be suitor much too old and much too dark.

Her overbearing mother must have been taken aback by her normally mild-mannered daughter refusing to consider the proposal. She must have been even more surprised, shocked even, when the fisherman from Vieux Fort came asking for permission to court her daughter. I imagine it was a match she couldn't fathom, much less consent to. After all, they were well-respected people of substance, so how could they sanction their cherished daughter, an only child into whom they had poured all their hopes and aspirations, tying the knot with one no better than a "wharf rat" without

Magna a memoir of the enduring human spirit

a dime to his name, making a mockery of their investment in their daughter and turning them into the laughing stock of Desruisseaux.

Now, I can see the appeal of why the sheltered country girl, my grandmother, would have fallen for the tall, engaging, worldly young man who I suspected cut a striking figure. But what I fail to understand was how the demure, soft-spoken and conforming damsel was able to summon the courage to defy her parents, her overbearing mother especially, acting against their wishes and marrying this man whom she must have known was considered below her social standing and, as her parents would not have failed to mention, could not provide the standard of living she was accustomed to?

Did her courage come from being so smitten by and in love with this man her parents obviously regarded as an upstart? Or did she see him as her knight in shining armor who would rescue her from the yoke of her overbearing mother and from getting hitched to a man she didn't fancy and found way too old and way too black? Or did she know that, secretly, her father wasn't all that opposed to her choice and so took courage? Or could it be that all along inside the damsel lay an unsuspecting resolve of steel?

Hard to tell. But despite the odds and parental opposition, the couple married on Sunday 6 January 1924. As far as the biblical command, be fruitful and multiply, is concerned, this union would be a match made in heaven, for it would produce eighteen offspring (thirteen surviving into mature adulthood) and, as of 2024, over 230 living descendants scattered across the globe.

Ancestors

But when Jonah Francis placed the wedding ring on the finger of his beloved Marie and promised *until death do us part*, I'm pretty sure he couldn't have imagined the struggle and hardship he would endure in Desruisseaux caring for his wife and tribe.

His tribulations began from the word go. He forsook all he knew—fishing, the sea—to arrive in a distant hinterland as an outsider, a stranger, looked down upon because he was without a sliver of land and not much of anything else for that matter. Yes, he was marrying into property, but since his powerful mother-in-law, who likely held the reins of the wealth, hadn't taken too kindly to him joining her family, she was begrudging in her support, even though that meant hurting her only daughter, her only child.

How did an acolyte turned boat boy turned fisherman become a farmer? When did he learn to farm? His stay with the priests in the presbytery and his stints as a boat boy and fisherman would have ill-prepared him for the life of a farmer. But distant from the sea and occupying land that required little teasing to yield its bounties, my grandfather had no choice but to take up farming.

Once established in Desruisseaux, farming wasn't all my grandfather did. He weaved rope from the bark of the *maho piman* tree to sell, kept bees, worked as a carpenter, which included carving *kannòts*, reared animals, and occasionally went to sea. Uncle Mano said that 6 AM never found his father in his bed. He worked six, seven days a week, from sunrise to sunset. He hardly ever had sufficient time to sit down and eat a full meal; eating was having a bite on the run. All this, yet my grandfather wasn't even a man of robust health. He was sick off and on throughout his life, but

Magna a memoir of the enduring human spirit

no sooner did he recover from an illness than he was back to the grind.

Even my grandfather's benedictions contributed to his hardship. He was blessed with a wife as fertile as the land he was cultivating, but her bountifulness, which for the longest time excluded boys, meant many mouths to feed but no boys to help ease his workload, as was the custom of the time. Listening to Uncle Mano describe my grandfather's arduous life, it occurred to me that the biblical proclamation, *By the sweat of thy brow thou shalt eat bread,* captured Papa Jonah's life perfectly.

And as if Papa Jonah's troubles weren't enough, my uncle told of a certain Winfied who was Papa Jonah's nemesis. Winfied was married to one of Pappy Ambroise's daughters, who was thus Mama Jonah's aunt. Like Papa Jonah, Winfied hadn't brought much of any property into the marriage, but he was from the Desruisseaux area and married to a more direct line of Pappy Ambroise (a daughter as opposed to a granddaughter), so he was higher on the pecking order and thus more entitled than my grandfather. At least, that's how Winfied and the community saw it. And if anyone missed that message, Winfied made sure they got it. Always in the saddle, a pipe in his mouth, permanently wearing a stern countenance, and dressed in a khaki outfit with a hat to match and knee-high rubber boots, he was the spitting image of the much-feared *kolonms* (overseers) or *Massas* (owners) of the sugar plantations of old. Rarely did he step down from his horse when conversing; he mostly spoke to people looking down astride his horse. It was as if Winfied had inherited the throne of Pappy Ambroise. However, people feared him not just because of his

Ancestors

severe countenance, or his *kolonm* or *Massa* bearing, but also because they believed he had *gadès*, obeah men, protecting him and doing his bidding. I wouldn't even be surprised if people suspected that he was the one who had put obeah on Papa Jonah to deny him sons. So no one dared touch Winfied's property. His bananas and other fruits stayed rotting on their vines or branches if he did not harvest them, and no one risked tying their animals or letting them stray on his land.

This was the man who chose no other person than Papa Jonah, a man up to his neck in struggle and tribulations, to harass, humiliate, and show who was boss.

Winfied would closely monitor the progress of Papa Jonah's garden, and just when it started to bloom and show signs of bearing, he would let loose his flock of sheep and goats into Papa Jonah's garden, turning all his labor to naught.

Uncle Mano said Papa Jonah would fume with rage, and he would sharpen his cutlass fine, fine, fine, and all the while saying something like, "I tired of taking, this is the last straw, mark my word, this time I will make Winfied *tann èk konpwann* (hear and understand), I chopping him thin, thin, thin."

By then the entire household would be in turmoil. Children crying, children screaming, "No, papa! No, papa!" Children hugging their mother, imploring her to make Papa stop. After all, as wicked as Winfied was, he was family; he was married to their grandaunt.

According to Uncle Mano, next thing you know, as if to see for himself the full damage and misery of his mischief,

Winfied on his high horse, pipe in mouth, cutlass at his side, would come visiting Papa Jonah.

No sooner does Winfied arrive than Papa Jonah forgets all his vexation and promise of violence, and greets him like a long-lost brother with whom he can't wait to enter into fellowship.

"*Konpè, sa ou fè? kouman ou yé? Vini, vini pwan an bwè.* Friend, how you do? How are you? Come, come take a drink."

Winfied would take the drink but would never dismount his horse.

After he leaves, Papa Jonah, by way of explanation, would say something to the effect that Winfied is lucky he, Jonah Francis, has so many children to take care of; if not for his children he, Jonah Francis, would have seen to it that Winfied was dead and buried a long time ago.

One of the few ways Papa Jonah amused and unburdened himself of the responsibility of feeding his tribe and from the aggravation of men like Winfied was occasionally to join the company of drinking and gambling men. As soon as they heard "Jonah Francis get inside," which was how he announced his arrival at rum shops, everyone—rum shop owners, idlers, drunks, gamblers, free-loaders—knew they were in for a treat. Because regardless of whether Papa Jonah had a winning or losing hand that day, he would buy drinks for the crowd as if he were intent on getting rid of his money as fast as he could. His name changed. Desruisseauxnians called him *Abondans* (abundance).

I don't know how, with his hands so full, Papa Jonah found the time and energy to wander around. But gambling and free-spending weren't his only vices. He fathered at least two children—Rachel and Matthew—out of wedlock. My mother said that in her innocence and ignorance, all the time her father was giving her ground provisions and other fruits of his labor to take to Rachel's mother, she never suspected anything, which shows how clueless children long ago were. Uncle Mano said he was pretty sure Mama Jonah had suspected her husband's affair with Rachel's mother because when she brought lunch in the forest for him, she would meet them there chatting.

The story of Matthew, Papa Jonah's other outside child, is slightly different. Papa Jonah was a good friend of this man called Popo who took leave of his wife to work in French Guiana. While he was away, Papa Jonah visited his home frequently, ostensibly to check on the welfare of his wife who was pregnant with (as people thought) her husband's child. After Matthew was born, Papa Jonah visited with greater frequency. But it was only years later that people put two and two together and realized that Papa Jonah was Matthew's father.

NOTWITHSTANDING Papa Jonah's wandering eyes, my maternal extended family, the Francis family, is close-knit and places a high value on family togetherness, even down to the fourth and fifth generations. I have often wondered how my grandparents were able to instill in their children such a strong sense of the importance of family sticking together, looking after each other. How were they able to crystalize in their children family togetherness as a virtue. Rarely would any subset of the Francis family meet without dwelling on the importance and necessity of the family sticking together.

Magna a memoir of the enduring human spirit

Uncle Mano said Papa Jonah was the main one responsible for this family trait. He was constantly hammering in his children the value of family togetherness.

I can picture the Francis family gathered on a Sunday afternoon under the shade of a mango tree next to the house amidst bird calls, burbles of the nearby *wavin* (brook), and distant voices of neighbors, the air infused with the aroma of flowers and ripening fruit. Some children sat on the long bench next to the tree, some standing, some crouching. They are jostling and teasing each other, barely paying their father any mind. But while to them the family gathering is all fun and games, to him it's a matter of life and death, the whole purpose of his existence, his back-breaking work keeping his family afloat. And so he begins his pep talk (in Kwéyòl) and the emotion and urgency in his voice compel the children into attention.

My children, always hold hands, make the family work. If you grow apart, you will become weak, but if you stick together, you will grow strong. Tolerate each other, forgive each other, don't be too sensitive, don't let little misunderstandings rip the family apart. In the long run, in the grand scheme of things, it is family that's important, it is family that matters. My children, the only thing I ask of you is to hold on to each other.

My uncle said that Mama Jonah also played an essential role in propagating family togetherness, for although she wasn't as big on making speeches, she made it her duty to introduce her children to all her relatives and to make the rounds visiting relatives with them.

I was in London in 2017, launching *The Stall Keeper*, my third book and second novel, when one of my aunts, the

Ancestors

sixth child of Mama Jonah, residing in London, died at 81. About a week before she passed, her doctor had informed her children that she didn't have much longer to live, so if they desired communion with her, they should do so soon. As my aunt's children and their spouses and her grandchildren gathered at her hospital bedside to receive her blessing and last words of admonishment, hooked to IV tubes and red-dialed monitors, her message to them of caring for and tolerating each other and staying together as a family wasn't far from the message my uncle said Papa Jonah had constantly hammered into his children.

I reckoned the loneliness, insecurity, and lack of a support system associated with being an orphan or an only child must have induced in my grandparents a heightened sense of the importance and value of family, which propelled them to pass on this family togetherness meme to their offspring, and, like genes, this meme is being passed on from one generation of Francis to the next.

Papa Jonah died (and was buried) on Tuesday 8 March 1966, after a prolonged bout with prostate cancer. His death and burial certificate said that he was 77 years old, but according to some of his children, he was in his mid-sixties. My mother was 37. I was only eight at the time, so I don't remember much about the events surrounding his death, except that there was a lot of talking and commotion and people moving in and out of our house.

Mama Jonah soldiered on without her husband for almost two decades. She died of cancer on Wednesday 12 November 1985 at the age of 82. She lived long enough to meet most of her grandchildren and some of her great-grandchildren. And she would no doubt have been pleased to know that as of 2024 her descendants had multiplied to 58 grandchildren, 100 great-grandchildren, 89 great-great-grandchildren, and three great-great-great-grandchildren.

My mother and her siblings spoke about their parents in very reverential terms. They quoted their sayings and admonishments with almost the same degree of sacredness or reverence that people quote the Bible. Listening to them talk about Papa and Mama Jonah, you would swear they were referring to deities. They brought to mind the ancestor-worship practices of some African and Asian cultures in how they revered and paid homage to their ancestors. Maybe my mother and her siblings' veneration of their parents is another factor that has helped keep the Francis family togetherness meme alive and well, and maybe, assuming my brother and his wife were correct, the ancestors were rewarding my mother for her and her siblings' fealty by allowing my mother to commune with their ghosts.

And what would the ghosts of Papa Jonah and Mama Jonah be telling my mother, I wondered? Unlike Gill and Ma Gill, they wouldn't have been as impressed with the bountiful numbers of the Francis line. After all, none of their progenitors have birthed and raised as many children as they did. But they would have been pleased with how the family has stayed together, even down to the fourth and fifth generations. I imagine them telling my mother, "Magna, you have worked hard all your life; rest your little body, my child. But hold on, don't let go; you are the strongest of all our children. But Magna, make sure you tell your children and grandchildren that now it's their turn to keep the family tradition of togetherness going. Make sure you tell them that."

CHAPTER FIVE

Desruisseaux

DESRUISSEAUX is the ancestral home of my mother and her siblings, the ancestral home of the Francis Family, the Papa Jonah and Mama Jonah clan. It's a place firmly imprinted on the first (my mother and her siblings) and second generation (their children) of the Francis'. No matter how far we roam, what corner of the globe we reside in, how long we have lived away, or how many children and grandchildren we have, home to us is Desruisseaux. I won't be surprised if, when my mother lay bedbound, her mind roaming freely, Desruisseaux, where her *lonbwi* is buried, was its most frequent destination.

Desruisseaux is a rural hamlet tucked inland a few miles from the island's Atlantic coast, between the rural communities of Belle Vue to the West, Anse Ger to the East, Vigier to the South, and Blanchard and Ti Rocher to the North. In larger geographical terms, Desruisseaux occupies the southeastern corner of the island and is part of the Micoud South electoral constituency, sandwiched between the Micoud North and Vieux Fort North constituencies. It is about 30 miles or an hour's drive to the capital (and largest) city of Castries, but Micoud, the nearest town, is only about

Magna a memoir of the enduring human spirit

4 miles or 12 minutes away to the Northeast, and Vieux Fort, the second closest town, is about 7 miles or 20 minutes away to the south.

Desruisseaux is part of a southeastern interior farming belt stretching from Belle Vue in the South to Mon Repos and Praslin in the North, but inclusive of Mahaut, which represents one of the island's most fertile and productive agricultural lands. The belt's rainforest canopy is home to the Amazona Versicolor, the St. Lucian parrot (Jako), endemic to St. Lucia, and its designated national bird.

Desruisseaux, meaning many streams, is a rich, fertile land that, besides possessing many springs and *wavins,* is traversed by the Canelles River and the two branches of the Ger River. Therefore, it is unsurprising that Desruisseaux likely started as a sugar plantation, but about 1885, in the time of Pappy Ambroise, my mother's maternal great-grandfather, no sooner had the Desruisseaux plantation exited the sugar business and become idle land, than a settlement of squatters, comprising initially some 40 cottages and accompanying gardens, sprang up on the land and thus probably began the establishment of Desruisseaux as a settled community.

At the time of my mother's birth in 1929, Desruisseaux was an isolated community, reached (and people got around) primarily by foot, horseback, or on carts drawn by horse or donkey, along footpaths variously cutting across farms, rivers, *wavins,* and forest. A public pathway linking Desruisseaux to the coastal highway took one to Micoud, Dennery, and Castries in the North and Vieux Fort in the South. But it was probably poorly maintained, and the shortest and likely quickest way of accessing Vieux Fort or Micoud was along footpaths.

Desruisseaux

My mother's marriage certificate listed her domicile as Delomel, which can be considered part of or adjoining Desruisseaux. To get to Delomel, the vale or *fond* (valley, bottom) of my mother's birthplace and childhood, one would have had to take a footpath off the public pathway passing through the center of Desruisseaux, go down a two-hundred-yard steep slope to a *wavin,* cross the *wavin* and climb a gentle slope to a slight plateau on which sat the family dwelling. Beyond the plateau, the land sloped steeply down to another *wavin* into which flows a spring gushing out from the bottom of the slope in a part of the vale called *Wavin Kann* (sugar cane stream). Beyond the *wavin,* the land rises as if into the heavens.

The homestead was part of a 20-plus-acre parcel of land acquired by Pappy Ambroise and inherited by his five children, including Sylfide Ambroise, who became Ma Gill, my mother's grandmother. The Ambroise Vale lay between the two *wavins* mentioned above and stretched across the landscape. As an only child, Marie, my grandmother, who would become Marie Francis or Mama Jonah or Ma Jonah or Ma J, inherited her mother's share of roughly five acres of the Ambroise estate, which became the core of the homestead on which my mother was raised. Besides this five-acre parcel, Mama Jonah inherited from her father seven acres of thickly forested land, called *gwan bwa* (dense forest*),* in the vicinity of Blanchard, about two miles northwest of her homestead.

Mama Jonah inherited another parcel of land (about four acres) from her father, Gill Derose. The story goes that Gill gave his stepfather, Pappy Ambroise, money to buy a plot of land at *Wavin Kann* adjoining the eastern boundary of

Ambroise's land. Apparently, the purchase wasn't accompanied by a deed of sale since no such record was found. However, everyone in the area acknowledged and respected Gill's ownership of the land, which Mama Jonah inherited.

To this day, representatives of the descendants of Pappy Ambroise have continued to occupy their inherited portion of the original Ambroise estate. Thus, my mother grew up surrounded by Mama Jonah's cousins and aunts. The Francis homestead occupied a swath of land that began in one *wavin* and ended in the other and was surrounded by the homesteads of Mama Jonah's relatives.

When I hear of the biblical Garden of Eden, what comes to mind is the Mama Jonah homestead in Desruisseaux. In the immediate surroundings of her house, she cultivated an exuberant flower garden of all sorts of flowers —roses, sunflowers, orchids, day lilies, anthurium or flamingo flower, bougainvillea or paper flower, bleeding heart, golden trumpet, angel's trumpet, bird of paradise, chenille plant or monkey tail, firecracker or fountain plant, hibiscus, ixota or flame of wood, oleander or rose bay, plumbago, poinsettia or painted leaf, and turks cap or sleeping hibiscus. All around the house, beyond the flower garden, was an orchard and garden of all manner of fruit-bearing trees and plants—mango, plum, golden apple, papaya, avocado, cashew, breadfruit, breadnut, pineapple. The aroma of the flowers mixed with that of ripening fruit was intoxicating. If you ever wondered how a family could feed a dozen or more children in those times of economic hardship and backwardness, there is your answer—living off the land. To leave the Desruisseaux thoroughfare and walk down the steep path to the Ambroise Vale and the Mama Jonah homestead was to enter a whole different world that hints at the world when it was first created. It was the kind of place of beauty, tranquility, and purity that some would travel far and wide to inhabit.

However, to some, the vale was just bush, a place "behind God's back" to stay away from as much as possible. I understand that sentiment and can't help but be sympathetic. I who grew up in Vieux Fort, the island's second-largest town, had the luxury of romanticizing the vale. But the story was quite different for people who grew up there. The water table in the vale was never far below the surface, so with any little shower, one would have had to tread in sticky, clayish mud up and down the steep slope that took one to the Desruisseaux road and the outside world of church, school, and shops. One would also have had to trek down and up a couple hundred yards of steep slope fetching water. If Desruisseaux was regarded as countryside, the vale was considered a backwater, *anba bwa*, under the woods. Long after Desruisseaux had electricity and running water, the vale was still in darkness and without potable water. Only now, a vehicular road (dirt road) connects the vale to the rest of Desruisseaux.

Indeed, the distinction between rural and urban, countryside and town, was so sharp, and the disadvantages of living in the countryside so pronounced that, for example, many families residing in the Vieux Fort hinterlands of Grace, Belle Vue, Cacoa, and Vigier kept a house in Vieux Fort town so they could overnight or spend the weekend when they were attending church and other functions, and when taking their produce and other goods to market.

It is no wonder that back then town and village folk (children especially, no matter they were half-starving) used to look down on rural folk, calling them country bookie or *neg maron,* which once referred to runaway slaves, but now understood as ignorant, behind the times, *what a shame living in a place without electricity, running water, storefront windows, and street corners at which to hang out at nights.* Rural children visiting or attending school in urban areas were no doubt made to feel inferior and were under pressure to conform to the ways of what they would perceive as city-smart kids.

But not anymore. The joke is now on the city folk. Because Desruisseaux and most other rural villages and hamlets now enjoy the same modern amenities as the towns and coastal villages, and with an extensive road system reaching the far corners of the island, ubiquitous telecommunications and public transportation, and a high incidence of private vehicles, the advantages of living in the coastal population centers have eroded, but the disadvantages, including traffic congestion, land scarcity, rising crime, and lack of community cohesiveness, have meant that rural villages or hamlets like Desruisseaux are increasingly becoming the preferred places to live and the envy of city folk.

I'm glad for the Desruisseaux community and for my aunts and cousins who still make there their home, but I'm afraid that with its pristineness and wholesomeness and recent accessibility, the Ambroise Vale will soon be transformed into a housing development, a village unto itself, thereby banishing my notion of a Garden of Eden to a thing of memory. I have expressed to my aunts, uncles, and cousins my desire for the homestead to remain in its pristine state, devoid of development, the way it was when Mama Jonah lived there, when my mom lived there. But I know I'm fighting a losing battle. One cousin on the other side of the Ambroise family has already divided her family's portion of the vale into house lots for sale.

This is now. But back in the days when my mother and her siblings were growing up, or not even as far back as that, even in the days when I was growing up, Desruisseaux, especially the Ambroise Vale, was a place to run away from as soon as one was able to. Yet it remains imprinted on the Francis Family as home, which leaves me wondering whether the practice of burying the *lonbwi* (umbilical cord) under a tree (golden apple or coconut) soon after birth has something to do with the Francis' attachment to their ancestral home. If so, it lends credence to my mother's Igbo ancestors' belief that the *lonbwi*-burying ritual helps cement one's spiritual and communal ties to the land.

Come to think of it, though thousands of miles away, my mother's Igbo ancestors would have been quite at home in Desruisseaux. Like Desruisseaux, Igboland is a region of moist, tropical broad-leaved forest where agriculture abounds, with yam, cassava, taro, corn, melon, okra, pumpkin, and bean playing the leading roles. Bounded or traversed by such mighty rivers as the Niger (third longest in Africa), Cross, Imo, and Anambra, as well as being home to several lakes, including the Oguta, the largest lake in Nigeria, Igboland is also a land of many waters.

Magna (age 20) and St. Brice (age 26) getting married

CHAPTER SIX

Saving the Day

ALTHOUGH MY MOTHER didn't attend secondary school, she was nurse, doctor, and savior to her immediate and extended family, a beacon of hope and fortitude to her wider community, and her home was a sanctuary.

When we were children, she waged war against the roundworms that made a home in our intestines. Periodically, she gave us doses of vermifuge, a greenish fluid dewormer that was the most bitter and vile thing I have ever tasted. We dreaded the time when we had to take vermifuge. But it was very effective. A few days after taking it, we passed out so many white intestinal worms, the size of giant earthworms, coiled in our stool that an onlooker would have been forced to wonder how our tiny stomachs were able to house so many worms and how we could still be alive?

Often, when my mother's nephews and nieces from the countryside came down with one sickness or another, they were sent to live with my mother for healing. In Vieux Fort, they had the benefit of the nearby hospital and health center, and they escaped the cold and dampness of the countryside, which were thought to prolong or even worsen certain illnesses. Others, especially her younger brothers and sisters, came to give their aging and weary parents relief and to avail themselves of an education, for while the Vieux Fort Primary School was just a stone-throw away, children living in Desruisseaux had to take walk paths across rivers and forests to get to the Micoud Primary School, three to four miles away.

My mother often told of one of her nephews who came to live with her as a toddler, most likely because he had fallen ill. At the time his speech was not yet fully developed, so when someone came visiting, he would pull on my mother's dress to say the visitor was a woman and on his pants that the visitor was a man. But despite his astuteness, he was left befuddled when his mother visited. He stared back and forth from his mother to his aunt, unable to decipher which was his mother. Now, it wasn't that the sisters closely resembled each other; my mother was much taller and bigger than her sister. So I suspect it was their voices that confused my cousin, for all the sisters sounded alike.

Although my mother was very engaging and conversational, she wasn't a touchy-feeling kind of parent; displaying physical affection wasn't her strongest suit. She was a no-nonsense, tough-love kind of person, all action and taking charge. Her love was revealed in her dedication and commitment to caring for her family, keeping them safe and healthy, and going to great lengths to put food on the table. And let's face it, when you have so many children under your care, where are you getting the time to be lovey-dovey with them?

The best time to experience the soft side of my mother would be when you fell sick in her care. Then she would

Saving the Day

be at her warmest, most attentive and compassionate, and go out of her way to serve your favorite dishes. Unfortunately, when sick I was in no position to enjoy the dishes. I can recall one such time when I came down with measles. Out of greed, I gulped down some delicious pumpkin soup, only to throw up all of it.

Procrastination wasn't part of my mother's vocabulary. She addressed problems, repaired things, and took care of business promptly. Her punishment of her children was swift. She straightened out people, put them in their place, at the very moment they were aggravating, displeasing her. She was the opposite of my father. He would let a lot of our misbehavior and disobedience slide until they accumulated and built up to the point where he couldn't take it any longer, and then he would beat us in a rage. Not my mother. It was as if she were there with a whip in hand, waiting and hoping for us to mess up, or, in the words of the *Sudden Impact* character, Harry Callahan, telling us, "Go ahead, make my day."

My father was undoubtedly the primary breadwinner of the family. After all, for the most part, my mother was a stay-at-home mom. But with my father busy sewing, farming, beekeeping, transporting bananas and passengers, repairing and maintaining his vehicles, and preaching and conducting Seventh-Day Adventist crusades, essential and time-sensitive matters could easily fall through the cracks. Besides, he was a procrastinator. His banana plants would need propping, but he would wait and wait, so by the time he finally got around to propping them, many of them would have fallen, laying to waste months of labor. We would inform our father of needing money for a school field trip, and he might never respond, leaving us to conclude he didn't want us to go or he didn't have the money, only to dig his hand in his pocket days after the field trip had come and gone to hand over the money. Very often, it took considerable nagging from my mother to get my father to replace some rotting board in the house or fix one thing or another. Of course, I have realized that I'm also a procrastinator, and my youngest sister has informed me that procrastination is a common trait in men, for her husband is no different from her father in that regard.

My hardworking and weary father may have been the family's primary breadwinner, but in matters of urgency, my mother had to take things into her own hands. She couldn't leave such matters to my father. She was therefore the clincher, the guarantor that the affairs of the family would take center stage; that while she and her husband were engulfed in the bread-and-butter struggle for survival, their eyes were kept on the prize. With great diligence, aplomb, and relentlessness, my mother was the one who ultimately safeguarded her children from going astray, ensured they were adequately fed and clothed and stayed healthy, and saw to it that education didn't pass them by. True, my father earned the bulk of the household income, but often it was the pennies my mother generated from her ceaseless industriousness that pushed the family over the hump of staying afloat, of being able to cater to the basic needs of her children.

Genesis 3:19 says: *By the sweat of thy brow shalt thou eat bread.* Now, it seems the Christian interpretation of that text was that God was punishing Adam with hard labor for eating the forbidden fruit. But my mother didn't read it that

Saving the Day

way. To her, there was nothing called hard work; there was nothing punishing about work; on the contrary, what many thought of as hard work was to her a blessing, a pleasure. My mother approached work with enthusiasm, with gusto. Curse or not, she would have it no other way.

She left no stone unturned to make ends meet. To supplement the family income, she baked bread, sold ice, manufactured icicles and ice lollies, helped my father process and bottle honey, and turned her deep freezer into a business where people paid to preserve their fish and meat. She transformed her rocky, uphill yard into a bountiful garden. When the yard ran out of space, she went aerial: she built boxes in which to grow lettuce, onions, carrots, and cabbage, which always brought to my mind the Hanging Gardens of Babylon, which I must say had nothing on my mother's yard garden. On Sundays, she led the charge to the farm to harvest the family's weekly supply of fruits and ground provisions.

One of my mother's favorite sayings was, "I have never seen work kill anyone." And it seems she had never heard of the proverb: *All work and no play makes Jack a dull boy,* but had certainly taken to heart Proverbs 16:27, *Idle hands are the devil's workshop; idle lips are his mouthpiece.* So, as children, we could never be relaxed around her; we could never be at ease. She didn't suffer idle hands. We were her carpenters making the seedbed boxes, her laborers tilling and weeding her garden, collecting dirt from construction sites, animal manure from the pasture, and seaweed from the Atlantic Ocean to turn her stony yard into a miracle garden; we collected and brought in the firewood to bake the bread, and were her sales task force selling things like icicles. So strongly my mother ingrained the habit of discipline and constant work in her children that I can't spend more than half a day relaxing without feeling that I'm wasting my life away.

However, thanks to my mother's dedication and commitment to work, her home never lacked food, those around her never went hungry, and her children were too occupied and too fatigued to stray far off the straight and narrow path. The value of discipline and hard work was another one of the lessons my mother's life exemplified.

In the 1970s, my mother decided to speculate in gold. She travelled to Guyana to purchase gold jewelry for resale in St. Lucia. She probably got the idea from an older sister who had migrated to Guyana in the 1950s but had since returned to St. Lucia and then moved to the US Virgin Islands. As an inter-territory speculator, my mother was following her Igbo ancestor's tradition, and more generally West African tradition, that continued in the West Indies with enslaved women taking the surplus of their provision plots to market and, after slavery, to an interisland huckster trade where the women traveled on board schooners to other islands to buy and sell produce and other goods.

After each trip, my mother was overflowing with stories about the people and situations she encountered, about how she talked customs officers (sometimes putting them in their place) out of charging her duties on the gold, or the creative ploys she employed to evade such charges.

My mother's stories made her Guyana travels out to be a great adventure, and upon her return, we, her children, were entertained for weeks. But her Adventist brothers and sisters were not as amused. Adventists, at least those in St.

Lucia, were not allowed to wear jewelry, so as a gold speculator my mother was promoting or enabling a practice frowned upon by her religion. To the church, her new venture was no different than an Adventist operating a rum shop—a definite no-no. And it made matters worse that we, the Reynolds family, had an exalted position in the church: my father was a much sought-after preacher and was invariably the church elder.

Unsurprisingly, the pastor preached sermons that seemed to target, to reprimand, my mother's unkosher enterprise. So much so that for a while, she, one of the very pillars of Adventism in the south of the island, stopped attending church.

Now, knowing that my mother would have been aware of the possible church fallout from her gold speculation, yet she wasn't dissuaded, and the lack of any overt sign of opposition from my father led me to conclude that at the time the family was facing severe financial difficulties that my mother's enterprise was helping to alleviate. If so, it presents yet another example of my mother scaling mountains to keep her family afloat, to save the day.

I have this overriding image of my mother donning short pants pulled over her stomach that seemed perpetually with child, getting ready to, or in the middle of, battling to put food on the table, getting her children in schools, safeguarding them from the evil of the world, moving heaven and earth and then some to ensure they amount to something in life.

My brother, who gave my mother's eulogy (and also my father's before that), has intimated that our mother was a feminist without even trying, without giving the matter any thought, and probably without even being mindful of the concept. I agree with him totally. Although my mother was a stay-at-home mom, her contribution to feeding and keeping the family afloat, especially in terms of effort and proactiveness, was equal to and, in some instances, surpassed her husband's.

How MAGDALINA, my youngest sister, and I were able to attend secondary school provides an excellent example of how my mother's astuteness, diligence, timely intervention, and refusal to take no for an answer saved the day again and again.

The story began on September 14, 1970, when three new junior secondary schools opened their doors. One in Vieux Fort, less than a hundred yards from my home, another in Micoud, and the third in the southwestern town of Soufriere, about twenty miles northwest of Vieux Fort. All three schools were donations of the Canadian government. During their construction and the few months before they opened for classes, the schools generated plenty of excitement among prospective students and their parents.

And who could blame them? Before this Canadian goodwill, there were just four secondary schools on the island—St. Mary's College, St. Joseph's Convent, the Vieux Fort Secondary School, and the Seventh-Day Adventist (SDA) Academy. It wasn't until 1974 that the Castries Comprehensive Secondary School, another Canadian donation, opened its doors to become the island's fifth full-fledged secondary school. So it went without saying that these new schools were significant additions to the island's education system. The schools were called junior secondary schools

Saving the Day

because they offered the first three of the five years of secondary education, which could then be completed at a full-fledged secondary school, such as the Vieux Fort Secondary School (renamed Vieux Fort Senior Secondary School to differentiate it from the junior secondary school, and later Vieux Fort Comprehensive Secondary School).

The Vieux Fort Junior Secondary School was built on a hill overlooking the Caribbean Sea and included four buildings that formed a rectangle enclosing a small playground. Although I had taken the entrance exam for the school and, with great anticipation of attending, had kept a close watch on its progress, from the time bulldozers leveled off the site to the day when green chalkboards, which I had wrongly thought were movie screens, were placed in the classrooms, I almost didn't set foot in it.

I had taken the entrance exam for the school, but I never received my exam results or an invitation to attend the school. But exam results or no results, name on the school roster or not, my mother sent me marching to the Vieux Fort Junior Secondary School in my brand-new school uniform as though my name was the first on the school roster. I arrived to find the school swarming with children. Groups from different villages and towns were already staking their turf. There was a long line of students ahead of me waiting to register. When my turn came, the teacher, Teacher Ryan, told me my name wasn't on the roster, so I should go back home, and he can't be expected to admit everyone who just walks in off the street.

I was almost in tears, but while waiting in line, I had overheard the teacher asking a boy who was also from the Plain View School whether he was a good footballer. When the boy answered "yes," the teacher registered his name. With that knowledge, rather than returning home with my tail between my legs, I told the teacher I was a very good footballer and played on the school team with the other boy from the Plain View School.

The teacher smiled. Among other duties, he would serve as the physical education instructor for the school and, therefore, the soccer, cricket, and track and field coach. Knowing there would be soccer, cricket, and track and field competitions among the three junior secondary schools, he kept an eye out for athletes. He needed the best teams he could get.

"What position you play?" he asked.

"Full back."

"Yes. Yes. Aren't you Mr. Reynolds's son, the *Semdays?*"

"Yes, sir."

He nodded and mumbled, "Well, Mr. Reynolds, we will see, we will see," and he wrote my name on the roster. I was in.

When I returned home that afternoon with the news that the school admitted students even if they had not taken the exam or their names weren't on the roster, my mother was presented with a solution to a problem that must have been bothering her for quite some time. Two years before, when it was time for my sister to sit the entrance exam for the Vieux Fort Secondary School, she couldn't go because the exam was held on a Saturday, and it was against our religion to study or write exams on the Sabbath. To my parents, everything, even education, took second place to God. After all, He said: *Seek ye first the kingdom of God, and his righteousness; and all these things shall be added*

Saving the Day

unto you. To make matters worse, by the time the junior secondary schools came around, my sister had passed the cutoff age, so she wasn't allowed to sit the entrance exam.

On the second day of school, bright and early, my mother with my sister matching her stride, entered the compound of the school that promised a solution to her problem. She said that when she opened the door to the headmaster's office, he was in mid-conversation with a teacher informing him that Room Three, her homeroom, was filled to the brim with students. Paying no mind to the teacher's discouraging report, my mother stood quietly at the entrance of the headmaster's office until he waved her in. She explained to him how bright her daughter was, and the only reason she hadn't taken the entrance exam was that the teachers at the Plain View School had said she was too old. But as she was coming to see the headmaster, she saw several students the same age as her daughter. This school, she told the headmaster, was her daughter's last chance to attend secondary school. The headmaster reportedly replied, "I will be the last one to deny someone an education. Please leave your daughter."

This was my mother at her best. She reveled in her ability to take charge of situations and turn them to her advantage when mere mortals would have resigned themselves to the hand of fate. She took great pride in finding the exact words at the right time to neutralize an enemy or potential enemy and have them eating out of her hands when mere mortals would cower. And she seemed to relish the retelling of the story even more, often embellishing it to emphasize her prowess. Well, her encounter with the headmaster was just one of many such tales. Right up to the time she fell ill, she was still recounting with gusto such defining moments of her life.

My sister's acceptance made my mother realize how easy it was to get admitted to the junior secondary school; it must have seemed to her a free-for-all. I can well imagine what was going on in her mind. *Why not add my second youngest child to the list? After all, he was just as prepared as his older brother for secondary school; they were in the same class at the 'Mission' School, and his grades were just as good or better than his brother's.*

So by the second week of the first school year of the Vieux Fort Junior Secondary School, my mother dressed my brother, Prosper, in the school's uniform and sent him to school as if no one belonged there more than him. Amazingly, her ploy almost worked. My brother was admitted; he attended classes for two days, even answering some of the teachers' questions when no other student could. But his luck ran out when the school conducted its first official schoolwide enrolment check. My brother was found out and sent home. To his great chagrin, he had to return to the Plain View School while his older brother and sister moved on.

I suspect being two years under the acceptance age he looked much too green to have gone unnoticed. To add insult to injury, a year later, when it was time for my brother to sit the entrance exam for the Vieux Fort Senior Secondary School (the last year of such entrance exams because thereafter all students would have to pass through the junior secondary schools), he couldn't take the exam because it was on a Saturday, the Sabbath of the Lord. Therefore, my parents were left with little choice but to send my brother,

Saving the Day

apparently their brightest and most educationally promising child, all the way to Castries to the Seventh-Day Adventist (SDA) Academy, which admitted students of all ages.

My brother recalled our mother leaving nothing to chance, walking him to take the 3 AM Monday Castries bus, and her heroic efforts putting pennies together to cover his weekly expenses. He vividly remembers how stressed she was on Sunday evenings when she could not secure sufficient food supplies or money to see him through the coming school week.

MY MOTHER WAS AS RELENTLESS in protecting her children against evil, against going astray, as she was in feeding, clothing, educating, and keeping them healthy. As teenagers, my mother's youngest brother (Uncle Mano) and her oldest son worked as footmen on my father's passenger bus, transporting people and cargo (loaded onto the bus's roof) from Vieux Fort to Castries and back. As footmen, their job was to load and offload the cargo. Uncle Mano lived with us at the time. He and my eldest brother were best friends: they did everything together, including chasing girls and going out at night to dances and the cinema. But there was a catch. As strict Seventh-Day Adventists, my parents didn't condone that kind of lifestyle. They imposed a strict curfew whereby everyone must be home before 8 PM. Many a night, my uncle and brother were locked out because they had violated the curfew and so had little choice but to sleep under the house among the herd of sheep and, most likely, toads, rats, mice, and what have you. The sheep got so used to sleeping with them that they accepted their company without a murmur. Uncle Mano re-

Magna a memoir of the enduring human spirit

counted that sometimes he would be dreaming of rain or of having a shower, only to wake up to find a sheep urinating on him.

My parents were alarmed. To them my uncle who was a Roman Catholic and thus unsaved, a heathen, was leading their son astray, undoing all their efforts at keeping their children on the straight and narrow path. Now, this didn't make much sense to me because everyone knew my brother was just as wayward as anyone else and was just as likely to be the one doing the leading astray. His waywardness, I suppose, started as a form of acting out, rebelling against my parents' abandonment of us (at least that's how it must have felt to their children) when they departed to England. Reports of my brother's unruliness, his going out of control, were part of the reason my mother had aborted her London stay to return home. Nonetheless, after time and again warning my uncle about coming home after hours, spoiling his children, leading them astray, my father said enough is enough, and gave my uncle some money and told him he had to leave and find his own place. My uncle said that all along he knew it was my mother, his sister, putting my father up to this. But unlike his brother and sister, who would pronounce my mother *méchansté* (wicked), that didn't bother him much. He let this slide like water off a duck's back and went his happy-go-lucky way.

Now, I think my uncle had gotten it right. My mother was behind my father's reaction to his coming home late and pairing with my brother to indulge in activities that didn't meet their approval. There was no mountain my mother wasn't willing to climb to safeguard the souls of her children. When I was growing up, it was my impression that

Saving the Day

when my father put his foot down, disciplining and punishing us, it was most often a result of my mother's prompting. His evening curfews and his whipping us when we went on the field to play ball, mixing with Vieux Fort's "ungodly children," were all due to our mother's instigation. My father who had to sew day and night, yet in between had to find time to keep bees, cultivate bananas, manage or drive his passenger and cargo truck, and lead the Vieux Fort Seventh-Day Adventist congregation, had little time and energy left to mind boys coming home late at nights, going on the playing field without permission, or reading novels considered not in keeping with his Christian faith.

Upon informing a neighbor (around my age) that I was writing a book about my mother, she recalled telling my mother that she remembered her from childhood as a strict disciplinarian and my father as a calm and indulgent parent. My mother laughed and laughed, and said, "If my husband wasn't doing it, then I had to be the one to do it."

Yes, my mother protested against some of the novels I was reading, books she thought were Satan's ploy to contaminate me. She collected all my novels, some of which I had borrowed from school and public libraries, and set fire to them. What choice did my father have but to go along with my mother? Silence, ignoring her, wasn't an option. She was relentless in reminding him, nagging him, to take action. Sometimes, I suspect my father went along just to get his peace of mind. Besides, it's not like he was opposed to or didn't see value in what she was urging. It's probably that, unlike her, he preferred to avoid conflict, confrontation, disturbances to his peace of mind.

However, I must hasten to add that my younger brother, Prosper, has a different recollection of my father's role in the burning of our books. He said it was his impression that our father was enthusiastic, even zealous, about novels corrupting us and ordered us to stop reading them and bringing them home. So in that regard, he didn't think our father needed any prompting from our mother. On the contrary, he remembered that our father was the one who made the bonfire and marked the occasion with a speech, which impressed upon him that while our father's natural inclination was to value books, he thought he was doing "God's work" in burning the books. According to my brother, the event made such a lasting impression on him that whenever he reads something or watches a movie featuring the bonfire of the vanities in medieval Florence, Italy, he recalls our father burning the pile of books. He even remembers that it was on a Friday evening just after we had welcomed the Sabbath.

I have no reason to doubt my brother or to assume that my recollection is sounder than his. So I'm drawn to conclude that when it came to safeguarding the souls of their children, our parents were in step with each other, were on the same page, and that there was likely more than one book bonfire.

SOME OF THE LESSONS my mother's life manifested came straight out of the Bible. In Acts 20:35, the Bible says: *It is more blessed to give than to receive.* Well, it seems my mother took this verse to heart. Her generosity is legendary, a trait she probably acquired from her father

Saving the Day

who was so generous that he was renamed *Abondans*. Everyone I meet, young and old alike, who knew my mother speaks of her generosity with a smile of relish on their face. They reminisce about the honey my mother used to give them, about stopping by my mother on their way to school, hinting that they hadn't had breakfast, so my mother would give them something to eat. A cousin, now in her fifties, who was raised in Desruisseaux, recently told me that when she was a child, my mother sent her mother, my aunt, a basket containing a cake (pumpkin cake more often than not) and fried flying fish and bread every Friday evening without fail. The cake and flying fish and bread had to be shared among many, so it was only a tiny share she would end up with, yet, for many a week, her small portion was one of the highlights of her week. Each week, she waited with great anticipation for Friday to come, and when the food basket arrived, she and her siblings stood on alert.

When we were growing up, we usually accompanied our mother to Desruisseaux on her visits to her mother and sisters who lived there. She never failed to shower her nieces and nephews with sweets on those visits. Of course, to children nowadays, candies are no big deal, but in a time when we were all poor, they were indeed a treat for us children. Some of my cousins fondly recall that when as children they visited my mother, she would make them do some work, would give them unsolicited admonishment that they didn't care much for, and would even preach her Adventism, but that was all okay, that was all right because they could rest assured that they would be fed.

Luke 6:38 says, *Give, and it shall be given unto you.* Well, isn't that the truth? At least in the case of my mother.

She received showers of gifts from nieces, nephews, siblings, her children, adopted children, and friends. So much so that when, after she passed, we were sorting out her things, we found plenty of gifts that she had never used, some of which she had never even opened. As she lay bedridden, when I entered her bedroom, she would jokingly ask: "Anderson, *ki sa ou pòté ban mwen*; Anderson, what you bring for me?"

I would retort, "But Ma Sido, it's you to give me. You lie there, not lifting a finger, but making much more money than me, who is on my two feet."

SOME YEARS AGO, long before my mother fell ill, she was there planting yet another fruit tree in her yard when a visiting friend said, "Why are you still planting fruit trees when you may not be around to eat the fruits?"

If I remember correctly, it was a *mango djouli* tree, one of the mangoes most sought after because its pulp, unlike that of some other mangoes, for example, *mango lonng* or *mango vè*, has very few of the fibrous threads that stick between the teeth, spoiling one's enjoyment. And its deliciousness, its wonderful sweetness and texture, remain the same whether ripened on the tree or picked green and put to ripe.

Perplexed, my mother answered, "Don't I have children and grandchildren? Don't they have mouths?"

Years later, she was still talking about her friend's misguided question. She must have been thinking, *since when have I ever lived just for myself? When was the last time I did anything for my sole benefit?*

Saving the Day

I'm glad my mom didn't listen to her friend's advice because four years after her death and counting, we still enjoy the fruits of the *mango djouli*. And alongside the *mango djouli* is a *mango palwi* that defies the laws of nature. It fruits in and out of season. As soon as it produces and sheds one crop, it flowers and buds the next. It bears so bountifully that I get tired of collecting mangoes and looking for people to give them to. Besides mangoes and herbal plants, her yard continues to produce guava, plum, sour sop, coconut, avocado, cashew, and moringa. My mother's legacy endures in more ways than one.

Her reaction to her friend's comment brought to mind the prehistoric movie, *10,000 BC*, in which an elder told the hero of the story that,

> A good man draws a circle around himself and cares for those within: his woman, his children. Other men draw a larger circle and bring their brothers and sisters with them. But some men, have a great destiny. They must draw around themselves a circle that includes many, many more.

And, of course, in typical epic fashion, the hero did just that. Through his bravery and selflessness, he led the charge that saved from bondage not just his betrothed and his tribe but all the tribes of his known world.

From this I inferred that a genuinely great person loves and looks after not just his family and his village but his whole tribe, all his people. This suggests that true greatness is achieved only through living a selfless life, only through devoting one's life to caring and helping others. Indeed, many of the renowned historical personas whose works and teachings continue to influence and shape our lives and our society were not war heroes or builders of empires but those who, like Jesus Christ, Gautama Buddha, Mother Mary Teresa, and Mahatma Gandhi, gave themselves selflessly for the betterment of humanity.

My mother not only look after her husband and children. She cared for her parents in their old age and gave refuge to her nieces and nephews, cousins, and younger siblings when they were sick, nursing them back to health. Indeed, my mother was the matriarch of the Francis family.

But the circle she drew around herself encompassed many more than the Francis clan. She kept an eye on not only her children and those in her immediate sphere but on all the children of her Adventist church and the larger community. She embraced them as her children. She led the charge in the church's community outreach program, Dorcas, as it is called, in which church members care for the sick, needy, and elderly. She embraced them as her people.

Luke 10:25-37 presents *The Parable of the Good Samaritan.* The parable teaches two profound lessons. First, you should love your fellowmen, your neighbor, as yourself. And second, your neighbor is anyone in need. My mother fed the hungry and the not-so-hungry, healed the sick, clothed the naked, sheltered the homeless, comforted the weary, admonished the wayward. And while she was at it, she even attempted to save a few souls, ambushing them with her Adventist tracts.

Saving the Day

Pastor Wentland Paul gives further testimony on my mother's community involvement and the breadth of the circle she drew around her. As the newly appointed pastor of the Vieux Fort Seventh-Day Adventist Church, he recalled his baptism into the church's Dorcas ministry. At the time my mother was the leader of the Dorcas committee. She warned him he mustn't wear a white or long-sleeved shirt, and he should come with cleaning supplies and wear gloves, rubber boots, and old clothes. In other words, she won't have him as a bystander, a spectator; she intends to put him to work, to get his hands dirty.

This particular Dorcas intervention targeted an older, bedridden man living alone and who had no one regularly looking after him. The pastor said that the house was filthy. Rubbish, feces, and cobwebs abounded, and everything was blanketed with dust. A nauseating odor of latrine permeated the air. Cockroaches, and he suspected, mice as well, were having a field day. As soon as he entered the house, he realized my mother's instructions had one critical omission—the wearing of a face mask.

Under the direction and supervision of my mother, the women swept, dusted, and mopped. They scrubbed and bathed the man, toweled him dry, and powdered him as they would a baby. The pastor, whose job was to bag and take out the trash, was surprised at the women's dexterity, the way they shifted the man's body to clean and bathe him. He was also amazed by how much the women had transformed the home and its occupant after two hours of intervention. The house was now smelling fresh and clean. The floor was disinfected and shining. Not a speck of dust or dirt could be found. The older man was smelling sweet and resting comfortably on fresh bed sheets and in clean clothes. With the transformation, no one would have guessed the once filthy state and awful stench of the house and the sickening, pitiful state of its occupant. And to cap it all, the women fed him a hot meal.

When the women were leaving, teary-eyed, the older man thanked them profusely. Pastor Paul later said that, as in this case, he was always touched by the gratitude of the people the Dorcas women had helped. Intent on community involvement and a hands-on approach to his ministry, he said that he couldn't have picked a more hands-on, a more rewarding community activity than the Dorcas intervention.

According to the Pastor, my mother's Dorcas activity was just one aspect of her community involvement. He said my mother was like a social safety net for the community. Schoolchildren and sometimes families would drop by for meals, groceries, ground provisions, and clothing. But she didn't cater only to their physical sustenance. Knowing the needs, challenges, and distress of those around her, she served as a pillar of strength and fortitude, providing emotional support and advice on how they could improve, change their predicament. And it went without saying that she never failed to see about their spiritual needs, inviting them to church and crusades, gifting them Adventist tracts, praying with them, calling upon the Almighty to take charge of their lives, and sometimes even inviting the church elder or pastor to lead these prayer and ministerial interventions.

Pastor Paul mentioned Brother Elias James, a pioneer of Adventism in the South of the island, who, as an older adult, could no longer live alone because he had become

Saving the Day

blind. So my mother took him in, adopted him, so to speak, caring for him and catering to all his needs. His church and government subsistence allowances were insufficient to cover his upkeep, so my parents had to make up for the difference.

The pastor also recalled his first conversation with my mother after becoming the Vieux Fort church minister. During this conversation, my mother told him that when the Vieux Fort church was being built, she was pregnant with her last child. As soon as she became pregnant, she and her husband started putting money aside for the *layette*—everything the newborn would need for its upkeep and comfort. But when the time approached for her to give birth, upon asking my father for the *layette* money, he told her that he had used it all to help advance the construction of the church building. The pastor said that as my mother was relating this story, she wore a smug smile, as if proud of the reckless dedication of her husband to the cause of God and as if indirectly schooling him on the importance and seriousness of his mission and the great sacrifices others had made for the church. Of course, I can also well imagine how much my mother had nagged and scolded my father for his foolhardiness, presenting yet another instance of him misguidedly putting the interest of others, the church in particular, ahead of his family.

My mother didn't attend college or secondary school. She didn't even have a full primary school education. She didn't have a professional career. She rarely worked outside the home. Yet she lived a full and accomplished life. She was on her feet almost every waking hour of the day. There was never a shortage of things my mother had to do; one was never bored in her company.

This made clear that in the process of saving the day, my mother's life exemplified yet another lesson: that the path to the most meaningful and fulfilling life doesn't necessarily have to do with formal education, professional career, status and position, but with living not just for yourself but also for others.

An internet search revealed that Magna, my mother's nickname, is associated with such terms as "great," "mighty," and "universal." I'm not sure how my mother came upon her nickname, nor that the person who gave her the name had these significations in mind. But clearly, in hindsight, my mother didn't disappoint; she did justice to the name. And regarding her proper name, Philomene, she didn't disappoint either. Derived from the ancient Greek words "phlos" and "mnos," meaning friend and strength, Philomene signifies "lover of strength" or "powerful love," traits of which my mother was a living embodiment.

Given my mother's industriousness and enterprising spirit, I'm inclined to believe the DNA ancestry test results that suggest her African ancestors were likely Igbo people concentrated in Igboland in southeastern Nigeria because Igbos are so renowned for their business acumen and entrepreneurial drive that, as the saying goes, it is almost impossible to find a lazy Igbo man or woman. And talking about women, my mother would have been well at home in Igboland, where women dominate the rural retail market, and trading was one of their main social and economic functions.

Magna (at about age 30) and her children a few months before her departure to London

An artist recreation of the photo above

CHAPTER SEVEN

The Moral of the Story

IN 2018, while spending time in New York, my cousin living in Queens invited me to accompany her and Uncle Umen, the oldest of Mama and Papa Jonah's two sons, to Resorts World Casino in Queens, New York. I'm not much into gambling, but I gladly accepted the invitation because I welcomed the opportunity to spend time with my uncle, who resides in the US Virgin Islands and whom I hadn't seen since 2009, and that was at a cousin's funeral in St. Lucia.

We were in the midst of a cold front. New York was freezing, dreary and uninviting, but with the heater on full blast, the car was cozy. As we headed to the casino, Uncle Umen and I struck up a conversation. He asked about his sister, my mother, and said he would go home to St. Lucia next year to visit her. But in the next breath, he castigated her as a wicked, evil person.

Fine, I'm open to criticizing everything under the sun, including my parents and even God.

So upon what evidence is my uncle basing such an extreme accusation against his sister, and to her son to boot?

The Moral of the Story

Well, back in his childhood, when his parents sent him to live with my mother to attend school in Vieux Fort, my oldest brother, several years his junior, fell when trying to hop onto a moving truck, and while on the ground the other boys hopping the truck stepped on him.

My uncle said he wasn't there hopping the truck that day because he had to babysit another of my mother's children. Yet when my father got the news, without asking any questions, he put some serious licks on him. He ran. My father ran after him. Finally, he went on the offensive. He pelted stones at my father. He didn't return home that evening but slept at someone else's home, and in the morning walked all the way back to Desruisseaux.

Now, since it was my father who dished out the punishment, why was this evidence of my mother's evil? Well, according to my uncle, at the very least, my mother should have intervened and found him another place to sleep that night or given him transport money for the return trip to Desruisseaux.

My uncle said that what pained him the most was that because of the altercation, which was no fault of his, he could no longer live with my mother, and so with no place to stay in Vieux Fort, his schooling was cut short, and that's why today he doesn't "have education."

If my uncle is telling the truth, he was wronged, and my parents had overreacted. But could you blame them? They could have lost their child, or he could have been permanently maimed. And since in the past my uncle and brother paired up to do mischief, my parents naturally concluded he was there with my brother hopping the truck, and in

Magna a memoir of the enduring human spirit

their eyes, being the eldest, my uncle had to shoulder the lion's share of the blame.

And yes, the incident appeared to have left my uncle with lasting scars on his memory. But even if it had been my mother who had whipped him, was this such an evil act to be retold to her son fifty-five years later with such vehemence?

Listening to what my uncle presented as evidence of my mother's evil, I thought, but which parent, which older sibling, which aunt, which uncle, which cousin hasn't committed at least one act of unkindness, one act of meanness, one act of abuse toward their younger charge? Can anyone raise their hand?

At the time I was so taken aback by my uncle's accusation that I didn't even put up a defense, but the expression of shock and disbelief that no doubt registered on my face must have spoken volumes. So as if realizing he hadn't presented convincing proof of my mother's wickedness, he jumped on me.

"But Anderson, I heard Magna took out your eye beating you, and now you're blind in one eye. *Pòdjab*, if you lose the other one, you will be totally blind. So don't tell me you, too, don't despise your mother."

I might have smiled or perhaps grimaced when he evoked that incident. "He well catch me," I thought. "This is very clever, for there's no way I could be happy with being blind in one eye, no way I could look kindly upon my mother while harboring the thought that she was responsible for the loss of my eye." It's an event that hardly comes to mind anymore, at least not in an overly emotional man-

The Moral of the Story

ner, but here he was, exploiting my misfortune to give ballast to his dubious accusation.

The "eye" accident was the outcome of a childhood disposition. Growing up, I always had an overwhelming itch to create, to build things, to initiate activities. I tried forming football and cricket teams and organizing corresponding matches. After reading the Sugar Creek Gang novels, I added forming a gang to my list of initiatives. As pre-teenagers, I and two younger cousins, my mother's nephews, living with us, took an interest in *cannots* and sailboats. So in keeping with my need to start things, to build things, I led them into chopping down a big gum tree and hollowing out the trunk into a *cannot*. However, one day, impatient with the progress of our *cannot* in the making, we took to sea on a shallop lying on the sandy beach of New Dock Bay.

That day left a picture in my mind—a bright Sunday morning with a faint hint of a sea breeze. The calm waters of the Caribbean Sea glistened under the spell of the sunlight. Bird calls fused with the constant sound of the tiny waves cascading on the sandy beach. To our right, a Geest banana boat straddled the finger pier built by the Americans during their World War II occupation of Vieux Fort. Straight ahead to the horizon, the silhouette of the neighboring island of St. Vincent, twenty-one miles away, beckoned us seaward. We imagined we were Christopher Columbus on his maiden Caribbean voyage, about to discover new lands.

But about fifty feet out at sea, a sudden gale picked up the sails, and the shallop glided into open waters. Before long, we were about to pass the end of the pier. We panicked and started screaming and shouting and waving for help. Luckily, a pair of homeward-bound fishermen came to our rescue. One came on board and guided the shallop back to the beach. I don't know how, but the news arrived home before we did. My mother, who, as far as I was concerned, never missed an opportunity to whip any of her charges, be they her own children or her nieces and nephews, was there waiting. She gave each of us a severe whipping.

Unfortunately, in my case, she ended up dishing out much worse than what she thought would have been a straightforward thrashing when the tip of the leather belt struck me in my right eye. *Murder. Blood everywhere. I was blind; I was dying.* At least that's what I thought, seeing or rather feeling all that blood. So could you blame me for screaming all the way to the hospital and throughout my stay there? I don't think it was out of pain. I don't remember feeling any pain. Just primordial terror. Fear my eyesight and life was over. The doctor dressed and bandaged my eye. I wasn't feeling any pain, but I continued to sob.

My eye remained bandaged for several weeks. When the eye was healed and the bandage permanently removed, my sight returned, but it was never as perfect as before. The injury had damaged the eye's optic nerve and led to a condition called glaucoma. The injury had also compromised the eye's drainage system, causing the buildup of eye pressure that I was told would further damage the optic nerve and my eyesight. The damage and glaucoma, I was told, were irreversible, but the application of Timoptic eye drops would reduce the pressure and thus arrest the deteriora-

The Moral of the Story

tion. But Timoptic or not, my sight in that eye gradually faded.

I stayed with the Timoptic right into my late twenties, but by then I was experiencing drowsiness as a side effect and suspected there might be other side effects that had not yet registered. So convinced that the eye had lost all vision anyway, I stopped applying the Timoptic. Without it, the eye pressure became elevated, causing headaches. But after a while, the discomfort and headaches became my new normal; I came to accept the condition and learned to live with it. Moreover, my regular jogging routine was helping to reduce the discomfort.

Subconsciously, I found myself aligning my head and sitting position to where I could use my good eye to the best advantage. I noticed that the good eye had compensated with the eyeball having permanently rotated toward the defective eye, and, in the process, I lost, I think, some peripheral vision. In hindsight, it seems a mistake to have stopped applying the Timoptic, which was reducing the rate at which the eye was going blind. For all the time I thought I was almost or already blind, I still had some peripheral vision in the damaged eye.

My uncle bringing up that incident was an astute move, but his timing was off. If he had brought this up thirty years before, when I was still sore about the whole ordeal, he would have gained traction with me. But by the time of our conversation, I had already gone through all the above; my eyes had already made their physical adjustments and accommodations, and my mind had already made the needed psychological modifications. I had already forgiven my mother, and memories or external reminders of the incident no longer induced self-pity, vexation, bitterness, or even fear of losing the other eye and being completely blind.

I told my uncle, "Yes, that's the truth, I'm blind in one eye, the right eye. Look, if you notice, the right eye is duller. It doesn't have the shine of the left one."

Yet I quickly added that the moral of the story isn't hatred but that we should not beat our children, not least because in beating them we can do permanent physical and psychological damage. I said that any one of us could have been killed, maimed, or blinded by any of our parents' many spankings because often they punished us in a state of rage. So if I must hate my mother because of my blind eye, then all of us should hate our parents because it was only by sheer good luck that more of us weren't permanently crippled or maimed in some way.

STEPPING OUT OF THE COLD, dreary evening and into the casino with its cozy warmth, alluring lighting, inviting card tables, flashing slot machines, and intermittent sounds of cascading coins announcing happy winners was like entering a magical world of bliss where all dreams were sure to come true.

I had fun at the casino. How could one not have fun in such an enchanting world? I even had fun watching my uncle play. He loves to gamble. A casino seems to be his idea of heaven. I got the sense that he had spent a lot of time thinking about the ins and outs of gambling. He had all kinds of theories about the best winning strategies to employ. For him playing the slot machines and other gambling games was serious business. He approached gambling like a calling, a devotion, an occupation, an art, a science.

Amid all the gambling, he was happy and generous. He insisted on giving me money to play the slot machines carefreely. He brought to mind Papa Jonah and his gambling and spending sprees. As my mother was fond of saying, "The apple doesn't fall far from the tree."

Watching my uncle gamble—a risk-taker, if there ever was one—also brought to mind what he shared with me on one of his visits to St. Lucia when I was still a teenager. He revealed that the only reason he had migrated to America was to rob banks because, from the Cowboy and Crooks movies he used to watch in St. Lucia, he thought robbing banks was a breeze. Only to arrive in America and realize robbing banks was no easy feat.

When he told that story, I laughed and laughed. But my laughter wasn't just about the hilarity of leaving your country and traveling thousands of miles to another country just to rob banks. You see, as a teenager, I had also contemplated a criminal life of robbery and drug trafficking. So it seems just as my uncle had watched too many cowboy and crooks movies, I had read too many Louis L'Amour and other Western novels. I even went as far as securing marijuana seedlings from a Rastafarian ganja farmer, which I planted in *Gwa Bois* on Mama Jonah's land at Blanchard. But heavy rain washed away the plants, and by then I suspect my parents' upbringing of us kicked in because I had switched my attention to pursuing higher education as a career path.

Despite my enjoyment of the time spent in the casino with my uncle and cousin, a few days later, upon reflecting on my uncle's accusation, I got vexed. In my vexation, I wrote a letter to the Francis family, part of which follows.

Family, who do you think my mother is? God? The woman had her first child at twenty and by twenty-eight had already given birth to and was raising seven children. Yet still, in that time of extreme poverty in St. Lucia, she had to take in her younger siblings as well as her nieces and nephews. When children in the countryside got sick, they sent them to my mother for healing; when they needed schooling, they were sent to my mother for education; when Mama Jonah's hands were too full, she found relief by sending her younger children to my mother. Now, this isn't a complaint, and I never heard my mother voice any such complaint. After all, this was nothing unusual in those days; this was the norm. This was how families survived. But still, give Jack his jacket. Wasn't that too much pressure to put on a relatively young person? If so, why do you expect her to have been perfectly normal, perfectly well-behaved, to have treated her charges with utmost consideration? She couldn't even give her own children proper attention, so how could you expect her to care unerringly for others?

So folks, the moral of the story isn't about my mother's wickedness or lack of wickedness at all, but that people need to take care of their own children. You make them, so take them with you wherever you choose to be. Raise your children yourself. If you don't, a lot of bad things can happen. And I need to provide no further details on that score because many of us, both the parents who left the kids behind and the kids who were left behind (myself included), have paid a heavy price.

In fairness to my uncle, his story wasn't the only cause of my outburst. Although more outrageous than most, his was probably just the last straw. Before him, one of my mother's younger sisters, who had lived overseas but now lives in St. Lucia, had presented on multiple occasions, particularly when she was tipsy, her own story, her own illustration of my mother's wickedness.

My grandparents had sent my aunt to live with my mother after her return from England, because maybe my aunt had become too much of a handful. By then my mother had eight children of her own, the last one born in England. What were some of the things my mother did to my aunt that made her, up to my mother's dying days, regard her as a wicked person?

First, there was an occasion when someone had carried false tales about her to my mother, and no sooner than she arrived home, before giving her time to explain, to defend herself, my mother beat her with an umbrella (no arguments there; this sounds like my mother).

My mother was a stay-at-home mom, but in her industriousness, she was always engaged in some activity to supplement the family income. One such activity was a small bakery. My aunt's second accusation of my mother's evil deeds stems from this enterprise. She complained that my mother used her, and not one of her own children, as her bread hawker.

The third accusation was that whenever she and my eldest brother got into mischief, it was her and not my brother my father used to blame. Yet my brother was the ringleader; he was the one instigating most of the mischief. And according to my aunt, my brother had always been bossy and big and robust for his age, so it's not like she could tell him what to do. On the contrary, if she refused to go along with him, being stronger, he would threaten to fight her or, worse, carry false tales about her to his mother.

In the fourth accusation, my aunt revealed that my father would give his two oldest children pocket change but wouldn't give her any. Instead, he would tell her she would get hers from her sister (my mother), knowing full well that her sister would do no such thing.

My aunt confided all this, often during conversations we had while having drinks on the veranda of her home. When she got into her diatribe about my parents, nothing could sidetrack her—not the incessant barking of the neighborhood dogs, the pungent fumes of nearby beverage factories, the oppressive tropical heat, nor the ever-present mosquitoes making themselves a nuisance.

Having listened on more than one occasion to my aunt's grievances against my parents, I wasn't surprised when one day, several years after my father's death but long before my mother's illness, before she became bedridden, my aunt paid my mother a visit, which I suspect wasn't so much to confront her but to gain empathy, to get an apology for the perceived wrongs, to help her move on, come to terms with the past.

When my aunt arrived, my mother was seated on a stretcher (her legs outstretched) on her veranda at her home on the St. Jude's Highway, taking a respite from the pun-

The Moral of the Story

ishing midday heat and incessant work, and enjoying her lush yard, orchard, and vegetable garden—all her handiwork rolled into one, and seemingly intent on giving the Hanging Gardens of Babylon a run for their money.

The din of traffic on the St. Jude's Highway and voices from a neighborhood pub and convenience store kept her entertained.

It had been a long time since my aunt had visited, so my mother was all smiles and warm greetings. She was no doubt looking forward to a long, sisterly afternoon chat and was probably thinking of what she could give her sister to take home. But her anticipated pleasure quickly soured when her sister opened the discussion.

My mother would have none of it. No more than the stench of the nearby commercial piggery, blowing across the veranda as my aunt talked. Not with her aversion to revisiting the past and her likely interpretation of her sister's attempt at parley as nothing more than an opportunity to make accusations and incriminations.

She quickly rebuffed her sister with something like, "Don't start; let the past remain in the past."

But here is the amusing thing. When I told one of my older brothers (who, from childhood, had displayed a reckless bravery I'm yet to see in anyone else) visiting from the U.S. about the altercation, playing peacemaker, he brought my mom to my aunt's home for them to make up. My brother said that, to his surprise, the sisters said there must have been a misunderstanding because they had nothing against each other, and they carried on as if they were each other's favorite sister.

Magna a memoir of the enduring human spirit

Aware of my aunt's gripe against my mom and that my mom was always complaining that she didn't know what she did to her sister, but her sister doesn't want her at all, I told my brother, "*Yo sé dé bann visyèz.* They are a band of two hypocrites."

But knowing my mom, I can picture what happened. She went there dressed nicely, all in smiles, carrying gifts from her garden or kitchen, and speaking in her softest and most compromising voice, even if she would still refuse to talk about the past. And my aunt, seeing my aging mother, the matriarch of the family, almost old enough to be her mother, in such humble countenance, didn't have the heart not to play nice. But, of course, that didn't stop her from griping about my mother afterward.

Unlike my uncle and his stupidity, I felt sorry for my aunt. I, too, had been in a similar position, seeking answers and explanations from my mother about my past, only to receive rebuffs or silence. I knew where my aunt was coming from. She was hurting. These were grievances she had been carrying most of her life, grievances she wanted to get off her chest once and for all. She couldn't help herself; she had to confront my mother and have a heart-to-heart talk with her, precisely what a therapist would have advised.

And it couldn't have been easy for her. This was a mountain of a sister, the matriarch of the family, whom some viewed in mythical terms, who was known to move mountains, squeeze oil out of rocks, snatch life from the jaws of death. The one everyone looked up to, the one (along with her family) who served as the standard bearer, the example others sought to emulate, and by whose standards they were judged.

And at this time, it's not like my aunt was a spring chicken and hadn't lived a life. She was well into her sixties, had been married once or twice, raised her children, made a home overseas, and now had reestablished herself in her homeland. Yet it seems that all along she had been carrying this burden and may have even concluded that the treatment she received from the hands of her sister when she was growing up damaged her psyche and colored her whole existence, accounting for a big part of her wounded self-image and the troubles and difficulties she had encountered in life.

Yet, I can't help but reiterate that both my aunt and uncle were missing the moral of the story, which was that children need to be raised by their parents. Take my aunt, for example. As a child, it was natural for her to think she was getting the raw end of the stick because she wasn't my parents' child, and this wasn't her home. Under the circumstances and given her immaturity, she couldn't help but think she was unwanted and was just being tolerated. After all, parents can always be expected to put their children first, and my parents' household was already bursting at the seams. However, other explanations for the way she was treated have little to do with her not being my parents' child, which at that young age she may have failed to grasp.

She was the oldest child in the household, so who else would my parents send to sell bread? Moreover, few children raised at my home escaped being pulled into whatever business enterprise or food production activity my mother was into, no matter how embarrassing or humiliating they might find them. As children, preteens and older, my mother had me, my younger brother, and a younger cousin living with us, going all over Vieux Fort selling icicles.

As a sales refrain, our pail of frozen icicles balancing in our hands, we used to shout everywhere we went selling, "*Sé moun-na, i; sé moun-na, ci; sé moun-na, i-ci-cles.* The people, i; the people, ci; the people, i-ci-cles." As a result, I acquired the nickname "Kyatt," as in Icicle Cart, and my cousin the nickname "Icicles." Today, when someone calls me "Kyatt," I know right away they are from my childhood. The last thing we wanted to be doing was humiliating ourselves hawking icicles. But with my mother, what choice did we have? If she can be considered evil for sending her sister to sell bread, how much eviler was she for sending her own children to hawk icicles?

Just as with my aunt and the umbrella thrashing, my mother had flogged me before I could explain my behavior or even utter a word. One such example stands out clearly in my mind. She sent me on an errand to a neighbor and upon my return she asked, "Who did you speak to?" But, for the life of me, I couldn't remember the person's name, which caused me to hesitate. Taking my silence as a refusal to answer and evidence of my rudeness, my mannishness, my mother put some serious licks on me, in the middle of which I miraculously blurted out the name that had eluded me, but my body was already on fire. So why did I get punished for no good reason? Was it because I wasn't my mother's child? Or was it perhaps because my mother was on edge, contending with her own stress, pressures, and frustrations?

My aunt mentioned my father blaming her for mischief spearheaded by my brother. But my father's policy had al-

The Moral of the Story

ways been to hold the oldest child responsible. My aunt may have been physically weaker than my brother, but she was older than he by several years, so in my father's eyes the blame and responsibility had to fall on her. As a child, I had been involved in mischief along with older brothers, but it had always been them my father punished while I got away scot-free because, according to him, they should have known better. They were older.

Finally, about not making a habit of giving his teenage sister-in-law money, could it be that my ever-cautious and risk-averse father was following the biblical dictate of abstaining from all appearances of evil? If so, how can he explain that to a naïve teenager?

One side of me was sympathetic toward my aunt; I felt sorry for her and thought my mother should have at the very least given her a hearing. But another side of me took offense and was uncomfortable with how my aunt had spoken of my mother in our previous conversations, sometimes in the presence of her children and, for that matter, anyone present. I thought it was insensitive, in very poor taste, and downright despicable for uncles or aunts to talk so disparagingly of their siblings to their siblings' children. To me, it is a violation of an unspoken code. Such baggage should not be transferred from one generation to the next.

Nevertheless, with my aunt, I had let this slide. She had an understandable gripe. But when this was followed by my uncle's accusations, I had to say, "Enough is enough." So in my letter to the family, I added:

Come on, Family, enough is enough. You think you were victims of my parents' mistreatment, but have you ever considered that my parents were even bigger victims, having to take on more charges even though they were up to their necks with their own children? Have you thought of that?

But Family, this isn't the main point. As I said earlier, these were the times all families had to squeeze up to accommodate one another. It was a matter of survival. So neither my parents nor their children can complain about the sacrifices they made for relatives. Just about everyone made those kinds of sacrifices. My mother herself had benefited from that practice. When we were growing up, she used to send us to Desruisseaux at Mama Jonah for summer vacation. And when she and my father went to London, she left us in the care of her father and one or more of her sisters. So this isn't the moral of the story.

What is the moral of the story?

Folks, the moral of the story is that once you are not being raised in your parents' home by your parents, you are at best a second-class citizen, and you are likely to attribute all treatments or punishments to the fact that you don't belong to the people raising you. Folks, there is a definite cost to not raising your children yourself. So if at all possible, keep your children tied to your apron strings.

Folks, I like objective criticism of anything and anyone. I am my mother's biggest critic. Part of the reason I can be my mother's biggest critic is because the mother-child bond was never fully formed between us, for it was severed when she left for London. This condition placed a certain distance between us that al-

The Moral of the Story

lowed me to be a bit more objective than otherwise. But she is one of the most industrious and proactive persons I have met. No matter the circumstances, she takes charge. She feeds the hungry, heals the sick, educates the unschooled, buries the dead, protects the vulnerable.

How many of us have done as much for the family as she has? How many have profited from her assiduousness, ambition, and take-charge attitude? Does that mean that no one has been hurt by her actions? Of course not; no one is perfect. How many of us have never harmed or hurt someone else? Is my mother to be blamed for everyone who didn't get an education, everyone whose life is considered by some a failure, everyone who has gotten divorced, everyone who isn't as wealthy and privileged as they thought they should be?

I completed the letter, but I stopped short of sharing it. I said to myself, *Anderson, why bother, why waste your time? This will just cause more vexation and bad blood in the family. It's not worth it.* The letter went no further than my computer.

Besides, I reasoned, this is life. In the arena of life, there are people like my mother who take charge, make the tough decisions and difficult choices; people who live in the moment, never shying away from the battle, putting out the fire and salvaging the furniture. And then there are the bystanders, the spectators. In the middle of the battle, they may praise and cheer on the heroines saving the day. But when things have quieted down, the danger has receded, the dragon has been slain, the bystanders become brave and heroic, full of plomb and bluster, and, forgetting the circumstances of the moment of decision and their timidity and no show in it, they are full of criticism for the movers and shakers.

My aunt should take comfort in the fact that my mother's refusal to entertain her complaint wasn't personal. In general, my mother has this aversion to history, to revisiting the past, to especially second-guessing her decisions. At thirteen, my head swirling and overflowing with family behavioral theories, I visited my parents' bedroom one evening to have a heart-to-heart, or rather a mind-to-mind talk with them to present my thesis on why different family members were behaving the way they did. My father quieted me down and told me that I was from a good family with good standing in the community and that I would be able to marry any girl I wanted. Meaning that I was from a privileged family, so I should "chill," I had nothing to worry about.

My mother, on the other hand, was visibly upset; she wanted no part of my nonsense. If not for my dad monopolizing the floor, she would have surely dismissed me with something like: "*Tibway, tiwé kò-ou douvan mwen èk maji-ou.* Boy, get out of my face with your nonsense." It was one thing for her to relate her stories, full of embellishments, most of which depicted her as the heroine saving the day, who put people in their place in no uncertain terms, but not history that hinted at or carried the risk of incrimination, or put her in a bad light. No way!

The Moral of the Story

One of my mother's sisters who was in England with her likes to repeat that when she told my mother, *"Eh-eh Magna, Anderson té ni chagwen-ou."* Meaning that I was displaying withdrawal symptoms due to my mother having been away in England. My mother would cut her short with, *"Betha, mwen paka palé about ich mwen.* Betha, I'm not talking about my children." Meaning that the past is the past; leave it there.

I've had problems with this aversion of my mother's to history. But the older I get and the more experience I gain, the more I understand and appreciate where she was coming from. Everything that happens happens in the moment, and it is only the moment that contains all the information—emotional, psychological, physical—that bears on a situation, on a decision, on an event. Outside of the moment, some of the information is invariably lost. Thus, the person living in the moment is likely privy to the most relevant information and is therefore best positioned to judge. Yet, sometimes, not even the person who was in the moment is fully qualified to judge because they may not have been aware of all the pertinent information, and, once outside the moment, they can't reassemble or recollect all the nuances of information that existed in the moment.

Late 1959, my mom left her seven children in the care of her father and sisters to join my father in England. On the surface, this may appear to be a terrible decision. But only my mother, who was in that moment, can fully appreciate the full circumstances, the emotional and psychological states of mind that weighed in on this decision. So, besides the guilt that may have accompanied her decision, revisiting it with third parties would surely place her at a disadvantage and would invariably minimize and trivialize what she had faced. If so, can we blame her for refusing to look back, even with her own children, on this aspect of her past? Will any answer or explanation satisfy us? Or will they sound to us like hollow excuses?

My mother reminded me of some of the heroines in Toni Morrison's novels, especially Eva in *Sula* and Sethe in *Beloved*. Having recently escaped from slavery with her children and faced with the imminent prospect of slave catchers returning them to bondage, Sethe proceeded to commit infanticide and thus protect her children from the unfathomable atrocities of slavery. Eva, on the other hand, arranged to have her leg mutilated and amputated, and thus qualify for a monthly pension to help save her children from destitution and starvation.

The cost continues even after the ultimate sacrifice, and those for whom the ultimate sacrifices were made are often ungrateful and reproachful. Beloved, the child Sethe succeeded in killing and saving from enslavement, came back as a flesh-and-blood ghost to haunt and reproach her. Her lover, Paul D, who shared her enslavement, said she loves too hard. Her two boys, having survived their mother's infanticidal intent and weary of their sister's ghost, ran away from home as soon as they were able.

My mother left for England to protect her sanity and to help prepare a better place for her children, yet she is blamed (I included) for the trauma her children suffered in her absence. She kindly took nephews, nieces, and younger siblings under her wings, but for her thank you she is vilified as evil and a dream killer.

The Moral of the Story

In *Sula*, which is set in Ohio between 1919 and 1965, to orchestrate her leg injury and amputation, Eva left her children in the care of a neighbor for eighteen months. The separation created a gulf between her and her children. Her daughter, Hannah, intimated that her mother never loved them: she never played with them as children and rarely displayed motherly affection. Of course, appalled, Eva retorted that she never had the luxury of being able to play with Hannah and her other two children, not when sickness, starvation and death were just one step away from her babies, not when they were under the constant threat of mouth sores, hookworms, and tuberculosis.

"...What you talkin' 'bout," said Eva. "Did I love you girl I stayed alive for you, can't you get that through your thick head."

The sacrifices you make for the ones you love are no guarantee that the love will be understood or returned. But *what greater love exists than giving up life and limb to save the life of the one you love?*

Magna (in her 50s) and her husband St. Brice
of over 30 years

CHAPTER EIGHT

The Making of a Matriarch

PNEUMONIA IS NO FRIEND of the elderly. According to medical research, up to 30 percent of elderly patients treated in a hospital for pneumonia die from the disease.[5,6] Despite having access to the best available medical care, it isn't uncommon for celebrities to die of pneumonia. In 2019, my favorite author, Nobel Prize Winner Toni Morrison, succumbed to the illness at age 88. The fact that at 87 my mother recovered from a severe bout of pneumonia, and I suspect if she had received timely physical therapy, would have walked again, resumed her life as before, and possibly lived past a hundred years, speaks to her strong, robust constitution, which arguably was a reflection of the conditions of her upbringing.

According to historians, the period of 1914 to 1940, encompassing my mother's birth and childhood, was one of "hard times" and "trial and effort." Thanks to the declining fortunes of the sugar industry, the Great Depression, government neglect, and the efforts of the plantocracy and their surrogates in government to deny the ex-slaves and their descendants access to land and other resources (all part of an effort to ensure a continued pool of cheap labor), most St. Lucians faced a harsh life of extreme poverty and deplorable living conditions.

Only about one-quarter of the population earned wages. Most people in the countryside walked barefoot except when visiting town or attending church, and even so walked barefoot to town, sometimes for several miles, putting on their shoes only upon arrival. As a common practice, instead of journeying with their shoes on, men tied their shoelaces together and carried their shoes around their necks. The story is told of a man who, when approaching town, broke his toe, but rather than cursing himself for not putting on the brand-new pair of boots around his neck, he rejoiced, "Ah, God has been good to me for had I put my boots on, I may have broken it instead."

Many people lived in crowded one-room or two-room wooden houses, rarely larger than twelve square feet, with the children sleeping on the floor on *kabann* (bedding of sacs and rags). Yet they were the more fortunate ones. Their poorer counterparts lived in *kay pay* (straw huts with dirt floors) as their ancestors did in the time of slavery. People may have been able to fill their stomachs, but because of unbalanced diets many suffered from chronic malnutrition. Diseases such as worm infections, tuberculosis, yaws, malaria (particularly in Vieux Fort), bilharzia, and venereal diseases (including gonorrhea and syphilis) were rampant and a direct consequence of overcrowded living arrangements, lack of potable water, poor sanitation and personal hygiene, and insufficient attention to prevention and early treatment of contagious diseases. In 1935, a medical officer reported that when urged to "clean your teeth," people retorted, "*Pa nésésè*, not necessary."

The Making of a Matriarch

In those days, children had to walk miles to school barefoot, and despite the great value parents placed on education as a means of overcoming poverty and raising their social status, school attendance was spotty or non-existent because parents could not always afford their children the food and decent clothing school attendance required, and many were forced to have their children skip school to help with the farm work or to take care of younger siblings.

People were only able to survive these harsh and debilitating conditions by growing most of the food they consumed, their use of folk technology (based chiefly on materials found naturally on the island), and cooperative self-help. The folk technologies, some handed down from the Amerindians who came before the Europeans, included clay pottery, charcoal making, canoe building, fish-pot and fishnet making, basket and broom weaving, *siyé bwa* (log-sawing), farine and cassava production, and hut building. The cooperative self-help practices, believed to be rooted in African traditions, included *susu or béja* (rotating savings group), *koudmen* (cooperative self-help), *jouné pwété* (trading labor), and a barter system. (Note, traditional Yoruba and Igbo Nigerian societies practiced *Esusu*, a rotating savings club akin to the St. Lucia susu.) These cooperative practices worked well in maintaining close kinship networks and keeping the use and need of money to a minimum, or making do without money altogether.

Wildlife such as birds and *mannikou* (opossum) from forest and woodlands, fish, *zandji* (eel) and crayfish from *wavins* and rivers, and crabs caught in swampy coastal areas after downpours were essential sources of protein. Meat in any substantive quantity was a rarity reserved for special occasions like wakes, weddings, First Communion and Christmas, when an animal or two were sacrificed for the occasion.

My mother's generation didn't only have to contend with an austere physical environment. They talked of a world populated with foul and mischievous supernatural beings who were just as likely to do them in, to threaten their existence. So much so that they considered it downright foolhardy not to secure protection against these evil beings. There was the *ladjablès* that came in the form of a beautiful, inviting woman who lured men into the woods for the sole purpose of getting them lost and having them wander in the forest, sometimes for days. Then there was the *maman de l'eau*, a mermaid, another beautiful woman, who surfaced nearshore and enticed men to follow her into deeper water and then wasted no time giving them a death by water. There were also the *jan gajé*, evil spirits, shapeshifters who came in different forms and guises, sometimes for the simple pleasure of scaring people out of their wits.

When I was a child, toads tormented me in my sleep. I would wake up each time screaming, "There is a frog in my bed." My family reckoned that a *jan gajé* was playing me mischief. However, toads inhabited the yard and under the house, so they could have entered through holes in the floorboard or open doors in the early evening. No toads were ever found in my bed or under it, but one night we did find a cat in the house, so taking no chances that it was a *jan gajé*, after killing it, my mom set fire to it in a bucket. Toads still visit me in my sleep, but with less frequency.

The Making of a Matriarch

My oldest brother said that our parents were convinced that I was *magoté*, meaning I was born with a sixth sense that enabled me to see evil spirits unnoticeable by others and which gave me protection against them. If so, the gift was both a blessing and a curse. The evil beings could torment my sleep, but could do me no real harm. And they must have viewed me as their nemesis; my very presence filled them with discomfort and vexation that I was untouchable and a source of reproach. Of course, though flattered, I'm not sure I believe in any of this, but my oldest brother, who also thought it plausible that my mother was in communion with ghosts as she lay dying, harbored no such doubt of my specialness.

As disconcerting as these supernatural beings were, they were not the worst this generation had to endure. The place was so teeming with evil spirits and persons intent on doing others harm that people felt compelled to seek witch doctors or, rather, obeah men called *gadès*, for self-protection. So much so that *gadès* played a central role in society. They didn't discriminate between good and evil. Their clients or patients were just as likely to visit for remedies and protection against harm as to procure curses, spells, and poison to harm others. Lovers came for potions to ensure their love interest remained dotishly in love with them. Some came for spells to scourge their enemies with incurable illnesses, crop failures or totally barren farms, sterile wombs, stillbirths, infant deaths, or retarded children. Others came for protection and remedies against such harm. Still others came to secure bountiful crops, acquire wealth, ensure their children excel in school. On top of all this,

Magna a memoir of the enduring human spirit

some people took matters more directly into their hands. They resorted to poison.

Among my mother's generation, stories of people suffering death by poison abounded. My mother and her siblings would not hesitate to present Papa Jonah as one such victim. Of course, as is usually the case with these oral narratives, each sibling had a slightly different version of the story. One version is that Papa Jonah used to go to sea with Dantes, a notorious *gadè*. He noticed that Dantes would never shit on land, so he innocently joked with Dantes, asking him how come he never poops on land. You see, Dantes was afraid someone would come after him and use his body waste to do him harm, as many believed he had done to countless others. Thinking that my grandfather was alluding to his evil dealings, Dantes took offense. A few weeks later, Papa Jonah started feeling ill, and he was spitting dark, unsightly mucus, and worms were crawling out of his scalp. He consulted a *gadè*. The *gadè* told him that he had been poisoned and asked if he had recently accepted food or drinks from anyone. Papa Jonah answered, "Yes, the other day *konpè* Dantes gave me a bottle of honey."

The *gadè* requested that he bring the honey to him. The *gadè* poured the honey on the bark of a breadfruit tree loaded with breadfruit in various stages of maturity; within a few days all the breadfruits and leaves fell off, and then the branches withered away. The *gadè* told Papa Jonah he mustn't worry; that he had a cure. He gave him a potion and told him that after he drank it, something would get caught in his throat. He should make sure he spit it out. He said that the potion would be the bitterest thing my grandfather would have tasted, but that is part of why it works so well.

The Making of a Matriarch

Papa Jonah did as he was instructed, and as the *gadè* had predicted, after swallowing the bitter potion, he felt something in his throat. He coughed and coughed and coughed, and just when it seemed that he would cough up all his intestines, something dislodged from his throat. He spat it out and noticed a spider crawling away. He stamped on it and crushed it to dust. After that Papa Jonah got well enough to work and carry on with his life, but he never returned to being a hundred percent.

In light of such stories, it should surprise no one that my mother was very cautious about eating other people's food. Eating at restaurants and street vendors was a no-no; she ate food only from close family and trusted friends. She may accept gifts of food from others but would turn around and give it away.

Even if you lacked faith in obeah men, you were advised to take a few precautions. To preclude harm to your garden, before planting, you were advised to drop a hat on the land and say the Lord's prayer, or sprinkle salt over the land, or dig a hole at each of the four corners of the land and put into three of the holes four grains of salt and cover the holes with lime. And to protect your house against *jan gajés* and other evils, you would do well to mix onion with your urine and sprinkle the mixture at the entrance to your home, and to occasionally burn in the house an incense composed of sap or gum from a cashew tree and bain joint, an ointment for arthritis available at the store. For ultimate protection, some people went as far as acquiring a *ti bolom*, their very own supernatural security guard in the form of a child with an oversized head.

Magna a memoir of the enduring human spirit

The living conditions of my mother and her siblings were no exception. They were raised in a two-room wooden house covered with *zésants* (shingles). Their parents slept in one of the rooms on a coconut-fiber stuffed mattress while they slept all together on *kabann* spread on the floor of the other room, which also served as the living room. They had no electricity, so they had to be ready for bed by 6 PM, but before bed they were sure to wash their feet and mouths properly or risk cockroaches kissing their lips and mice nibbling their toes while they slept. With no running water, their drinking water had to be fetched from the nearby spring, and bathing in the river or *wavin* or a rain downpour was the closest thing to a shower they enjoyed. Yet river bathing was the leading cause of the prevalence of bilharzia in the population, a disease that can cause anemia, malnutrition, and learning difficulties in children, and which after years of infection can cause liver, intestine, spleen, lungs, and bladder damage. More often than not, when my cousins from the countryside fell ill and came to live with us in Vieux Fort to recover from their illness, bilharzia was the culprit.

As school children, my mother and her sisters had to get out of bed at 5 AM, make one or two trips down the steep slope to the spring to fill their calabash gourds with water for refilling the large clay jars in the house. In the spring, they would likely meet children from the vale and beyond who were there for the same purpose. All children in the area eventually met at the spring. So it was a place of rendezvous and socialization, of fights and jostling to fill one's calabash, of teasing, taunting, and establishing a pecking order. My mom with her proactiveness, sharp tongue, and

The Making of a Matriarch

grand charge would have no doubt been at the top of the pecking order, even ahead of her sisters and children much older than her. She probably also ensured that her sisters were at the front of the water line. Such was my mother's sassiness and sharp tongue that grownups in the area identified or distinguished her from the other Francis children as "*sa ki fanm-lan*, the rude one." Before getting ready for school, my mother and her sisters also had to tend to the family's goats and sheep, untying and taking them to better feeding grounds.

Like most children of that era, my mother and her sisters went to school barefoot and without uniform. They attended elementary school in Desruisseaux from age five to ten and thereafter attended primary school in Micoud until they turned fifteen, the island-wide school-leaving age.

Their breakfast would entail *toloman* (arrowroot porridge) and cocoa tea; or a farine porridge; or warm breadfruit or cassava bread or sweet potatoes, with or without milk; or fried bakes and cocoa tea or bush tea. Lunch, which they often took to school in *carriers*, likely consisted of a *fufu* of farine and avocado, or any combination of breadfruit, plantain, green figs, ground provisions, with or without saltfish or sardines.

To get to the Micoud Primary School, they walked several miles across farms, rivers, and *wavins*. On the way, they were joined by other school children. Fights and quarrels were likely to ensue. My mother told plenty of stories of the battles she fought on the way to and from school, defending and protecting herself and her sisters against bullies.

But bullies weren't the only dangers or adversaries my mother and her siblings had to contend with on their trek to school. She said that one morning, on their way to school, as they were walking across a garden, they were attacked by a fully grown *bef mové* (mad cow), the largest and meanest bull they had ever seen. When the *bef mové* saw them, it stamped the ground with its hoofs, bent its head low, exposing the longest horns they had come across, and took after them with a vengeance. Luckily, there was a mango tree nearby. They ran for their dear lives to the mango tree and scrambled up. This infuriated the bull even more. He refused to go away. In vexation, he stamped the ground and horned the tree, saliva flying from its jaw. Petrified, my mother and her sisters had to wait until the bull's owner came and took him away. It was then, and only then, that they dared to venture down the tree and continue their trek to school. When my mother related that story, the picture that came to mind was of a fallen bull rider under attack by the bull he was riding.

My mother said that at school, she took to sweeping and keeping the classrooms spotless, such that some people thought she was there not as a student but as the janitor. As a result, the teachers and headmaster gave her special treatment.

My mother was like that. Her proactiveness bordered on manipulation. She said that when she did wrong and knew for sure Papa Jonah would spank her, she would anticipate his needs: wash and iron his clothes, cook his favorite dish, roast cashew nuts for him, or bring him water to drink before he had even made the request. Of course, her father knew what she was up to, but it worked every time because

The Making of a Matriarch

he just didn't have the heart to whip his daughter after all this pampering; after all, he was only human.

My mother took nothing for granted and left nothing to chance. As a guest at someone's home, be it that of a relative or friend, she would literally take over the duties of the house and perform so many chores—cooking, sweeping, dusting—that by the end of her visit, her host would be begging her to extend her stay.

When I was growing up, my mother had so many dreams whose interpretations were clearly that one or the other of her children was going astray, was getting into harm's way, that I became convinced that she wasn't having any such dreams, but was fabricating them as a manipulative tool to keep us on the straight and narrow path.

In those days, as if to match the austere living conditions, parents and teachers were very strict with their charges and didn't shy away from using the rod. And it was a time when children were truly raised by the whole village. They were taught to respect and obey elders, run errands for them when asked, and always greet them politely. It was often the case that any elder could whip any child in the community for misconduct and disrespect, and when the child got home, they were likely to get a second beating from their parents. At school, children were beaten for arriving late, giving wrong answers in class, fighting, using foul language, and other misbehaviors on and off school grounds. However, it is conceivable that all this beating and physical abuse in schools caused children to hate school, served as a learning mental block, and led to widespread truancy. For example, one of my cousins from Desruisseaux of my age revealed how this abuse and cruelty on the part

Magna a memoir of the enduring human spirit

of teachers caused him to detest school, and probably account for his never making much headway in school.

Returning home from school in the late afternoon, before they eat supper and get ready for bed, one on top of the other on the living room floor (where on any given night, they are likely to be visited by cockroaches, mice, centipedes, and other unwelcome creatures because the shingled, wooden hut was anything but pest proof), my mother and her sisters had to repeat the morning chores of tending animals and fetching water.

On weekends they did the family's laundry in the *wavin* into which the spring flows. They also walked the mile or two to Blanchard and descended the steep slope to the family *gwan bwa* (forest) land alongside which flows the Canelles River. There, against a backdrop of bird cries, the rustle of the forest canopy and the babbling of the river, they might spend a whole day bathing, cooking, catching and roasting fish and crayfish.

But the visit to *Gwan Bwa* wasn't all fun and games. They had to collect the family's weekly supply of ground provisions, including yam and dasheen, which they had to dig, and breadfruit, which they had to harvest by climbing the trees or using a gullet (forked pole). All of which they would have to carry on their heads, in large baskets or sacks, and retrace their steps up the steep slope to the Desruisseaux road, then a mile or two to Desruisseaux, then down the steep slope to the vale.

When school was out, besides their regular chores of fetching water, hand washing clothes, tending animals, and collecting ground provisions, they had to help Papa Jonah with his rope-making enterprise and cultivating and har-

The Making of a Matriarch

vesting his crops. In terms of their own money-making activities, they crafted brooms and weaved bags, baskets, and floor mats. The sisters also doubled up as sales agents. They carried the ropes, bags, baskets, mats, and surplus ground provisions in large baskets on their heads all the way to the Vieux Fort market (a three-hour walk) or the Micoud market (a two-hour walk). After selling their merchandise, they would purchase and carry back to Desruisseaux such essentials as saltfish, salt, butter, flour, sugar, cornmeal, oatmeal, cooking oil, and maybe some cloth.

In those days, for many St. Lucians, ready-made or store-bought clothes were out of the question; they were beyond people's means. So households had to either sew their own clothes or use the services of tailors and seamstresses, where payment was sometimes in the form of barter.

Fifteen was the primary school leaving age, so at fifteen my mother's formal education would have come to an end. As a school leaver, she would have thrown herself more than ever into supporting her father's farming and other livelihood activities, as well as her own income-generating endeavors.

My mother's family situation was exacerbated by there being as many as thirteen children to feed and clothe, a vulnerable father with self-defeating personality flaws who wasn't blessed with robust health, and a mother whose upbringing as a spoiled and only child ill-equipped her for raising such a large family.

Nonetheless, the children may have considered themselves fortunate, and they probably grew up with a certain degree of haughtiness and status, a sense of pride and

Magna a memoir of the enduring human spirit

dignity, and a better-than-thou attitude. Because as the great-grandchildren of Pappy Ambroise, a propertied, big man in Desruisseaux, and the grandchildren of the distinguished mulatto and propertied Jules "Gill" Derose, they had inherited or had access to as much land as they could use, and enjoyed some of the prestige and respect once bestowed on their forefathers.

The family certainly didn't lack entertainment, for my mother and her sisters were probably the most talkative and excitable bunch of people one would ever meet. When any group of them was together, it was perhaps easier to gain an audience with the president of the United States than to get a word in. And with so many of them, there was probably never a need to seek outside companionship. In that regard, they were self-contained, self-sufficient. Nonetheless, if they required additional playmates, there were the children of Mama Jonah's cousin, Pappy Ambroise's other great-grandchildren, most of whom lived in the vale.

It was a household crowded with girls, all vying for parental attention and special treatment. The family's meager material resources had to be shared among many, and given the absence of boys, the girls had no choice but to perform the traditional roles of both genders. Under these circumstances, I can well imagine the intense rivalry and one-upmanship, as well as the relentless upholding and defending of one's point of view that existed among the sisters in the crucible of the two-room Francis family home. I can also imagine the plethora of weapons of deception, manipulation, and verbal warfare that these conditions gave rise to.

The Making of a Matriarch

Is it any wonder that among the eleven sisters, with few exceptions, the only ones that got married and the marriage lasted till death did them part were those in which the husbands were as calm, quiet, and seemingly as docile as their wives were talkative, aggressive and confrontational? My father adopted the strategy of remaining silent even if my mother nagged all day. When visiting his farm in the hinterlands of Vieux Fort, he would be lively, whistling, sharing plenty of jokes and words of wisdom with the country folk, but no sooner does he arrive home, he falls asleep or perhaps pretends to do so.

Away from home, the husband of another sister was a leader of men. His circle of friends paid him deference, followed his lead, heeded his admonishments. But in the presence of his wife, he metamorphosed into an insecure child, smiling like an idiot at his wife's nagging and insults. I suspect that these men came to realize that to save their marriages and be around to raise their children, they had no choice but to let the women win the battle of words and sometimes the battle of wills, accommodate themselves to their wives' feistiness, their refusing-to-let-anything-slide personalities. The marriages of those husbands who were unable or unwilling to adopt this strategy invariably ended in divorce or separation.

However, I suspect that while the rivalry among the sisters was intense, when it came to the outside world they closed ranks and presented a unified front, defending the family from all real and imagined threats, preventing others from taking advantage of its vulnerabilities, refraining from discussing family business with outsiders, and refusing to entertain or participate in outsiders' criticism of the family. Papa Jonah's sermons and insistence on family unity may have helped deepen this, the closing of ranks, which in turn would have further cemented the notion of family cohesiveness.

It must have been heartbreaking to my mother and her sisters, knowing how their father toiled day and night, they walking all the way to Vieux Fort with loads of produce and other goods, the fruits of his and their labor, on their heads to sell at the Vieux Fort market, then walking all the way back to Desruisseaux, but no sooner they handed Papa Jonah the sale proceeds, he dresses up in his Sunday best— hat askew, handkerchief hanging from his pants' pocket, shoes polished to a shine—and pays a visit to his favorite rum shop and gambling joint, and upon announcing himself, "Jonah Francis get inside," wastes no time spending all of his and his daughters' hard-earned and well-needed cash, buying drinks for friends, foes, and strangers alike. Yet, to this day, I've never heard any of them breathe one word of criticism of him.

I think it was a testament to the spirit of the closing of family ranks and family togetherness that, despite my mother's talkativeness, she rarely spoke negatively to her children about her parents and siblings. Indeed, sharing that her mother was raised as a spoiled and only child was the closest she came to criticizing her parents. Can you blame someone who, after listening to my mother and her sisters talk about and quote their parents, mistakenly thought they were talking about deities?

Family togetherness aside, I imagine that growing up my mother had played a special role in her family. She was

The Making of a Matriarch

born in a household with a father who had to work from sunup to sundown to provide for his family, with no sons to ease the burden and little time for himself, much less time and presence of mind to run a family. It didn't help that she had a mother who apparently wasn't a take-charge kind of person by nature, and was raised as a spoiled and only child, and thus ill-equipped to raise a large family. Therefore, there was a take-charge vacuum or niche in the family waiting to be filled. My mother's sisters, especially the older ones, were probably just as hardworking and conscientious as she was. But it seems my mother was the one who most closely mirrored her grandmother, Ma Gill, both in terms of physique and bossiness. Moreover, being Ma Gill's favorite grandchild and the one spending the most time with her, she was most exposed to and influenced by her values and disposition. Thus, having the most wherewithal for taking control of family affairs, running things, holding it all together, my mother was the one who I think filled the take-charge niche and who, in time, would come closest to serving as the matriarch of the Francis family.

THE HARSH REALITIES faced by my mother's generation didn't mean that there was no fun and entertainment to be had. Indeed, as far as this generation was concerned, although they had a harsher life with fewer opportunities and conveniences and much less material comfort, they enjoyed a happier, healthier, and more wholesome life than later generations. In their minds, unlike the lifestyle of the present generation, which they view as a descent into vulgarity and discord, back then children obeyed and respected their parents and elders, and husbands and wives respected each

Magna a memoir of the enduring human spirit

other and stayed together for life. There was greater togetherness: people helped each other and were indeed their brother's keeper.

For entertainment, children trapped or hunted birds and opossums, bathed and frolicked and caught fish and crayfish in the rivers, played tug of war, hide and seek, jackstones, hoops, *cochi* (dice with split cashew nuts), wa-wa (a noise-maker), and more. The girls skipped rope and played with dolls that they fashioned out of cloth with stuffings of cotton or coconut fiber. The boys occupied themselves with wooden carts, tops, marbles, kites, and bamboo firecrackers and played a version of cricket called *woulé la ba*.

In those days, the gramophone and the talking machine (as radio was first called), much less television, were virtually absent. So much so that people came from far away to congregate at the few homes possessing these machines. But this didn't dampen or prevent adults from feting and having a good time. The absence of recorded music simply meant that for entertainment they had to create their own music (and even their own musical instruments), which usually took the form of folk bands with such instruments as the *tanbou* or drum, banjo, cuatro, violin, guitar, mandolin, *chak-chak* or rattle, *tibwa* or sticks, *zo* or bones, and *the gwaj* or grater. Or people simply got together and entertained themselves with storytelling and call-and-response singing.

Of the musical instruments, the guitar, violin, and mandolin were considered European in origin; the *tanbou*, *chak-chak*, *tibwa*, *zo*, and *gwaj* were considered part of the island's African heritage, but the banjo and cuatro were considered indigenous to St. Lucia because as far as anyone is aware these two instruments have always been made on the island.

At Christmas time, folks merrily went house to house in groups singing lustily, and in the spirit of the season the occupants of the houses expressed their gratitude with gifts of food and drinks. Wakes were rambunctious, all-night affairs with rum and strong coffee flowing freely, where inside the home the more somber mourners sang hymns. But outside, sometimes the more boisterous and inebriated mourners formed a circle, told jokes, performed skits, and, accompanied by a folk band, performed *konts* and danced *Kutumba*.

Perhaps of all the cultural and entertainment activities my mother's generation indulged in, the annual *Lawòz* (The Rose Festival) and *La Magwit* (The Marguerite Flower Festival) elicited the most community participation and were what most captured their imagination. Still in vogue today, but no longer the all-consuming community activity it once was, the flower festivals are an elaborate mimicry of colonial society and the unprecedented rivalry between the French and the English for St. Lucia. In this display of rivalry, *Lawòz* society represents the English and projects a colorful, exuberant, and rhythmic persona. In contrast, representing the French, *La Magwit* society is more subdued and melodic in its conduct. Both fractions exhibit the complete occupational hierarchy of colonial society, including royalty, soldiers, doctors, nurses, police officers, etc. The societies wage war by composing and singing songs that extoll their self-proclaimed superior qualities while deprecating their rival's. They may meet throughout the year where members sing or play folk instruments and dance. But once

Magna a memoir of the enduring human spirit

a year each society holds an elaborate day-long celebration (feast day) that includes morning mass, feasting, extended performances of singing, dancing, and the playing of folk instruments, as well as street parades with participants ostentatiously outfitted to represent the colonial occupational hierarchy. Indeed, the flower festivals present a synthesis of St. Lucian folk culture, accentuating its music, dance, storytelling, and cuisine.

The flower festivals, *Lawòz*, especially, weren't everyone's cup of tea. Many regarded them as contentious, bacchanal, *laydéyé* events not meant for decent folk. But Derek Walcott begged to differ; he saw great value in the celebrations. So much so that in a 2011 poem titled "The War of the Flowers" (dedicated to George 'Fish' Alphonse, another St. Lucian cultural icon and enthusiast of the Flower Festivals), he pays tribute to this iconic feature of St. Lucia's cultural heritage.

The battle of the flowers
is odorous and sweet;
they share each other's powers:
the rose, the marguerite.

The croton hoists between them
its flag of many colours,
no music for its emblem
no army like the others;

who with sharp shouts and answers
will march to fighting words,

The Making of a Matriarch

with admirals and commanders,
sashes and wooden swords.

But one thing that is curious
is that they never meet,
they are far, but still furious,
the rose, the marguerite.

Their clash is months apart
but soft each flower falls,
the rose with its red heart
the daisy's with its waltz.

With anthems loud and heated
and cries that dare defeat,
neither one is defeated:
the rose, the marguerite.

They are, as none supposes
together not apart;
violet is the daisy, the rose is
the banner of the heart.

Would that our scarred earth could contain
such a sweet violence
these flowers fighting to remain
not enemies, but friends.

Ah violet of the daisy,
no victory, no defeat;

their woundless wars amaze me,
the rose, the marguerite.

Unlike Derek Walcott, my mother almost never mentioned any of these cultural activities, so I presume that apart from the funerals and wakes of family members, she and her siblings were not allowed to attend or participate in these events, so they would have viewed these happenings from a distance, which speaks to how strict Papa Jonah and Mama Jonah raised them.

Magna in her 60s

CHAPTER NINE

Race, God, and Politics

JULY 2016, seven months before my mother fell ill and for the first time in almost 60 years a white man or an almost white man took the helm of government (prime minister), which some St. Lucians (especially stalwarts of the opposing St. Lucia Labour Party, SLP) construed as a return to the days of slavery and the days of colonial rule when the colony functioned primarily to serve the interest of the white plantocracy at the disadvantage of the overwhelming black majority. But I wouldn't be surprised if my mother didn't share the sentiments of the Labour Party about the new prime minister, Allen Chastanet, and his United Workers Party (UWP) because, for some reason, she was never enamored with Dr. Kenny Anthony, the former prime minister and then leader of the St. Lucia Labour Party. Besides, she never took a strong liking to or interest in politics. She mainly concerned herself with the things she had control over, what was within her powers to change, and that had a direct bearing on the well-being of her family.

Nonetheless, it was the Micoud South constituency seat with Desruisseaux, where my mother's *lonbwi* is buried at its center that Chastanet contested and won, which paved the way for him to become prime minister. So if the SLP stalwarts were looking for someone to blame for Chastanet's rise to the pinnacle of St. Lucian politics, they needed to look no further than Desruisseaux, my mother's home village.

But one should not have been surprised that Desruisseaux, the land of many streams, was the main instigator of Allen Chastanet getting elected. Since the formation of the UWP in 1964, only once has the UWP lost the Micoud South seat, and that was in 1997 when the Labour Party, under the leadership of Dr. Kenny Anthony, swept into power by a landslide victory that left only one UWP seat standing—Micoud North. So Chastanet opting to contest the Micoud South seat, which at the time his party had lost only once in its 52-year history, or about 12 general election cycles, was an astute move.

Desruisseauxnians, my mother's people, are a prideful lot who think highly of themselves and socially punch above their weight or hang their hats higher than their reach. For such a people, economic benefits aside, having the country's prime minister as their district representative would be a feather in their cap. It would be a great boost to their ego; it would put Desruisseaux on the map. Moreover, they had been spoiled by Sir John Compton, considered the father of the nation, serving as their district representative during his reign as prime minister. Sir John Compton, with his mulatto complexion, was just a shade or two darker than Allen Chastanet. So Desruisseauxnians were accustomed to voting for and likely preferred lighter-complexion representatives, which, if so, wasn't all that surprising because one legacy of slavery and colonialism is a psyche that views white people in charge as the natural order, their mere presence or involvement signaling greater value and importance. Thus, in more ways than one, Allen Chastanet as St. Lucia's prime minister and Desruisseaux's parliamentary representative would be a return to the village's glory days. Given all this, Chastanet opting to contest Micoud South wasn't just an astute move but a stroke of genius, for he chose the people most likely to overlook his color for the opportunity to host a prime minister. And maybe Desruisseauxnians didn't overlook Chastanet's race at all. On the contrary, if they place a premium on whiteness, then an almost-white prime minister as their representative would be an even larger feather in their caps.

The Labour Party did try to use the race card to hold on to power and keep Allen Chastanet as far from the seat of government as possible. Indeed, they referred to him as a "Massa," enslaver, implying that he thinks he is inherently superior to the people and linking him and his family to the days of slavery when his ancestors operated sugar plantations with enslaved labor.

As a rebuttal, Chastanet hinted that Kenny Anthony, the SLP leader, was in the same boat as him but changed his name from Barnard (the surname of his white father, David Barnard) to Anthony (the surname of his mother, Andrazine Anthony, of African and possibly Amerindian heritage) to distance himself from notions of slavery and thus become more palatable to the St. Lucian public. (Note: Kenny Anthony is just a shade darker than Allen Chastanet, whose mother, Julia Bird, is a white Irish woman; his paternal grandfather, Arthur Chastanet, was a Creole White; and his paternal grandmother, Iris Monplaisir, was a mulatto.)

Race, God, and Politics

In response, Kenny Anthony explained that, as an illegitimate child, it was customary for one to take their mother's surname and that the Barnards, his father's people, couldn't have been involved in St. Lucian slavery because they first came to the Caribbean from Sussex, England, in the 1880s, several decades after slavery ended.

The irony of this jostling for position to either link the other to slave-owing ancestors or to dispel any doubt of their ancestors' involvement in slavery is that if slave ownership ancestry were the basis for determining which St. Lucians care about the wellbeing of their country or which St. Lucians were fit to be prime minister, then many St. Lucians whom the census classifies as of African descent and who appear as black as people can be would fail the test because according to historians many blacks and colored St. Lucians owned enslaved people and sugar plantations. For example, in 1828, there were about 5000 free colored and black people in St. Lucia; they owned 2350 enslaved people (1202 plantation enslaved and 1148 personal enslaved) or about one-sixth of the enslaved population.[7]

Moreover, at the time, St. Lucians bearing such surnames as Francois, Goodman, Lansiquot, Monplaisir, Vittet, and d'Auvergne were all whites who more likely than not operated plantations with enslaved labor, which means that present-day St. Lucians with these surnames, although through miscegenation can no longer pass as white, might be just as "Massa" as Allen Chastanet.

Perhaps because of this knowledge the media didn't take the race card bait. Few, if any, journalists featured or reported on the race issue. And other than SLP zealots, the populace didn't take the bait either. They hardly mentioned or discussed it seriously. When the topic came up, some people's reactions were: "Well, Chastanet is not fully white," or "Well, if racist America can elect a black president, why can't St. Lucia elect a white prime minister?" Some others even voiced that the Labour Party should be ashamed of itself for invoking race to win the elections.

SLP stalwarts should not have been surprised that the people didn't play along with the race card. Most St. Lucians had no memory of a white St. Lucian politician, much less memory of the days when the white minority planter class and merchant elite dominated both the economics and politics of the country. As far as they were concerned, they had left their slavery past a long time ago and were enjoying a blissful life of racial harmony and tolerance. To them, racism was something that took place in faraway America and the once-upon-a-time apartheid South Africa. After all, the professionals and people populating most government and private sector positions looked no different than them, and, lacking the keen race or clorism consciousness of say, African Americans, they may not have noticed that the higher they climbed up the corporate or government ladder, the whiter the meetings they found themselves a part of.

Besides, white St. Lucians are so few, and most reside in secluded enclaves at the island's northern end that most other St. Lucians rarely come face-to-face with them and may be unaware that they still own a disproportionate share of the country's wealth. On any given day, white visitors far outnumber the native white population, and a non-white St. Lucian is far more likely to encounter such visitors than their fellow white citizens. One suspects that when encountering white St. Lucians, they are often mistaken for tourists or visitors on temporary work assignments. Furthermore, the evidence suggests that most St. Lucians usually choose to bury the past and let bygones be bygones because they find the history of slavery too painful and shameful to revisit.[8]

So by playing the race card, the SLP had barked up the wrong tree. As if taking a page from my mother with her aversion to revisiting the past, the people said, in effect, *Thanks, but no thanks; we are not going back there.*

Thus Allen Chastanet was able to brush off the opposition's racial barbs as easily as shooing away a bothersome mosquito. He rode to victory with an 11 to 6 UWP electoral majority to, as leader of his party, take his place as the 7th prime minister of St. Lucia. The racecard, it seems, had backfired. The party with the whiter party leader (Allen Chastanet) had prevailed over the party whose leader (Dr. Kenny Anthony) was a shade darker.

Sadly, in the latter half of 2020, as Chastanet's administrative term was winding down and the island was in the throes of another general election campaign, my mother was fighting desperately for her life. She passed away about seven months before voters could cast their votes to decide whether they were sticking with Allen Chastanet and his United Workers Party or switching to the St. Lucia Labour Party.

Yet I wonder what she would have made of all this racism talk. I don't know where she stood on the issue of race or racism; however, if her spirit or ghost came to visit, I doubt very much that racism would be a topic of discussion. Other than the racism she encountered in England, the subject rarely appeared in her conversations. I suspect a person's race or nationality was of little concern to her. She saw everyone, no matter what gender, size, age, or complexion, as an opportunity for engagement, for interaction. My mother was interested in the humanity of people and not so much their outward appearance. Besides, she had the knack of simulating the climate or atmosphere that works in her favor, that induces the most prejudiced of persons within her ambit to forget that they were supposed to dislike her. Yes, she would hint at gender double standards; well, sort of. For example (and that's the only one I can come up with), when watching television, she never failed to crack me up with: "I don't understand this television business. The men are always properly dressed, but the women are always half-naked." It cracked me up because I had to conclude that her assertion wasn't far from the truth. My mother, who, as my brother said in the eulogy, was an equal partner to my father in the Reynolds' family enterprise and more than held her own, may have been a feminist without even being aware of the concept. But a racist, no.

THIS WAS RECENT POLITICAL HISTORY, which is by no means the most heroic or prideful period in the island's history. On the contrary, viewing the island's recent politics as a travesty, many St. Lucians reminisce about their past heroic political figures (such as Sir George Charles, Sir John Compton, and George Odlum) but lament how low the nation's politics have fallen and have become disenchanted with government and politicians. For the island's most heroic epoch, we must go to my mother's formative

Race, God, and Politics

years when St. Lucia experienced revolutionary political changes.

In the mid-1930s, as my mother turned five, likely unbeknownst to her, the extreme poverty and deprived living and working conditions in St. Lucia and the rest of the West Indies set off spontaneous labor uprisings throughout the region with deadly consequences. Region-wide, between 1935 and 1939, no fewer than forty-six labor protestors lost their lives in clashes with authorities, 429 were injured, and thousands more were arrested and prosecuted. British warships docked at bay for the sole purpose of quelling labor uprisings became a salient feature of the regional landscape.

Although there were no fatalities in St. Lucia, during that period it too had its share of uprisings. On November 4, 1935, about 300 Castries coal carriers went on strike, prompting the governor to call a state of emergency and commission the services of rifle-armed policemen and the HMS Challenger docked at Port Castries. And in August 1937, island-wide sugar strikes led to the appointment of a commission of inquiry.

Being so young at the time, my mother was probably unaware of the uprisings, but they had far-reaching implications for the political and economic environment in which she would raise her children. In most islands, the spontaneous labor uprisings led to the formation of labor unions that metamorphosed into political parties. St. Lucia organized labor protests began with the formation of the St. Lucia Workers Cooperative Union, launched in 1939 and registered in 1940. George Charles, who was working as a timekeeper but who would become chief minister of gov-

Magna a memoir of the enduring human spirit

ernment, joined the Union in 1945, and his voice soon came to symbolize and champion the people's will for self-determination.

The movement that emerged from the uprisings induced Great Britain to grant universal suffrage to St. Lucia in 1950. Before then to participate in the electoral political process either as a voter or a candidate, one had to be literate and possess substantial income or wealth, which placed the limited politics that existed in the colony beyond the reach of the vast majority of its inhabitants. The following year, under the leadership of George Charles, the St. Lucia Workers Cooperative Union transformed itself into a political party, the St. Lucia Labour Party, and contested and won the 1951 general elections, the first elections under universal adult suffrage, the first elections in which the masses had a vote.

I'm not sure whether my mother voted in this historic election, but by then she was twenty-one years old, married, and had given birth to her first two children, Ezekiel and Ezildra. She may not have voted but she couldn't have helped hearing about the heroics of George Charles (whom many referred to as "*ti hach-la*, the small axe"), how in 1947 he led the Castries Bakery Workers Strike—the island's first union strike—and as an elected member of the Castries Town Board, he swayed the Board to designate the Choc Cemetery a common burial ground for all, thus doing away with the stigma of the paupers' section and starting the process of claiming the island for the majority of its people and dismantling its class structure. With subsequent constitutional changes and two more general elections, George Charles became the chief minister of government in

1960, and thus headed the first government of and for the masses of St. Lucians. As such, he has been credited with laying down the political foundation of the country and establishing the industrial relations framework upon which the nation was built.

MY MOTHER'S ORIENTATION toward politics was distant, but religion would play an intimate and significant role in her life. Born and raised a Roman Catholic, as was the overwhelming majority of the population, she was baptized in the Micoud Roman Catholic Church by Reverend Father Eugene Jaffus on February 9, 1929, when she was a mere twenty days old. In this sacrament of baptism, she must have been quite perplexed when Father Jaffus poured holy water over her forehead, naming her Philomene and pronouncing her a new Christian in Jesus Christ. At eight, clad in an all-eyes-on-me angelic white dress and veil, she joined a cohort of children similarly attired in a special 'First Holy Communion Mass' to partake for the first time in her life of the Eucharist Sacrament, the holy bread and wine, the body and blood of Christ, further cementing her membership in the Catholic church.

The sacrament of confirmation is the third and final sacrament of one's initiation into the Catholic faith. I'm not sure whether my mother partook of this sacrament, but if she did, she would have done so at the age of fourteen. In this ceremony, the bishop, most likely Archbishop Patrick Finbar Ryan, who would have come all the way from Trinidad to do the honors, would have traced a cross on her forehead with oil and with the words: "*Accipe signaculum doni Spiritus Sancti,* Be sealed by the gift of God the

Holy Spirit," imparted upon her the holy spirit and empowered her to go out into the world and spread the gospel of salvation.

Of course, all this changed in my mother's late teens. Then Adventism was embarking on the daunting task of establishing a foothold in the south of St. Lucia, an island where over 90 percent of the population was Roman Catholic, making it the most Catholic of the English-speaking Caribbean. And it seems my mother was among the first Adventist converts in the south of the island, probably the first in Desruisseaux and definitely the first of the Francis family. Having discarded her Roman Catholic robe, my mother got married in the Adventist faith, and together she and my father became the very pillar of Adventism in Vieux Fort.

As warriors for Christ, my parents disdained Roman Catholics as non-Christians, people of the world, instruments of Satan. They held them in contempt for worshiping idols, defiling their bodies with tobacco, alcohol, pork and other unclean flesh, for condoning the abominations of fornication and adultery, for refusing to keep the Sabbath holy, and for seemingly bestowing on pope and priest the status of God and the title of Heavenly Father. Adventists in St. Lucia, like my mother and father, did such a great job at painting Roman Catholics as ungodly and living in iniquity that when I gained greater exposure to Roman Catholics and their religion, especially in America, I was surprised to discover that many were just as or even more temperate or pious than the Adventists I knew back home.

CHAPTER TEN

Wars and Pestilence

COVID-19 found my mother in the middle of her illness. She saw people wearing masks, but I'm not sure she knew why or whether she understood that a worldwide pandemic was causing health and economic havoc. She was given neither the vaccines nor the boosters. But we insisted that visitors wear masks. One of her longtime friends, from the UK, refused to wear a mask when she came visiting, arguing that the coronavirus and the accompanying vaccines were a hoax designed by people like Bill Gates to control the world and to cull out those they deemed undesirable. I told her that, regardless of the validity of her politics, she couldn't visit my mother without a mask. She left in a huff.

My mother may have been unmindful of the COVID-19 pandemic, but in her long life she had seen or been affected by her fair share of calamities.

She was born between the two World Wars—eleven years after the end of World War I and nine years before the start of World War II. I never heard her mention World War I, but she recalled the mandated island-wide blackouts of World War II and the German submarine that had torpedoed two ships—the C.N.S. Lady Nelson and the Um-

139

tata—berthed alongside the Castries wharf, killing several people, all on account of some folks failing to fully observe the blackout stipulations. She even remembered a piece of the song children sang about the incident, which went like this: *The submarine coming, right in the harbor, to bomb Lady Nelson and torpedo Umtata.*

The attack on the ships was an unfortunate event, but it was a boon for many living near the harbor. They salvaged barrels of canned goods, flour, mackerel, and other items, which they sold cheaply, spreading the spoils to the population. Such was the bounty that songs of gratitude about the incident became popular—*God bless the Lady Nelson... Thank God for the Torpedo; it sank the boat and brought good things for the people of Conway.*

My mother also recalled the American World War II military presence in Vieux Fort, when the Americans transformed the Vieux Fort area into an army base, with the unintended consequence of turning the town into an overcrowded boomtown that boasted of rampant prostitution, easy money, and unprecedented high wages—"the good times." For many St. Lucians, the Americans represented their first encounter with paper money, and for some it was only after working for the Americans that they got to "know money," that they gained perspective on the value of their labor. Yet, if not for a policy directive of the plantocracy and the colonial government to keep labor discontent in check by restricting American wages and curtailing wage disparities, the Americans would have paid even higher wages. The American presence in Vieux Fort is believed to have inculcated a damaged culture of dependency and moral decay. So much so that for a long time after the

Wars and Pestilence

Americans left Vieux Fortians were said to be "sitting around waiting for the Americans to return and bring back the good times." The accompanying stigma and myth that "Vieux Fortians are lazy" persist to this day, which is ironic because my mother, considered a Vieux Fortian, was the hardest working and most proactive and dynamic person one would ever meet, and her children, all of whom were born and raised in Vieux Fort, are anything but lazy.

My mother related the story of the American soldier who shot dead a civilian worker and his dog as they entered the base because dogs were not allowed on the base. People said that when they arrived at the cemetery to bury the man, there was no corpse in the coffin. The incident would become the subject of *Ballad of a Man and Dog*, a play by essayist and playwright Stanley French, a member of the famed 1950s St. Lucia Arts Guild that sparked a cultural renaissance. My mother was probably unaware of the *Ballad of a Man and Dog*. After all, it was rarely staged. Allan Weekes, another member of the St. Lucia Arts Guild, is perhaps the only director to have staged the play, and only once.

When, after the war, the Americans (in 1949) dismantled the base, packed up, and left, Vieux Fort became a ghost town, causing Derek Walcott in *Another Life* (1973) to lament:

At Vieuxfort
the soldiers had broken up their base and gone,
the mustard-yellow bungalows through the palms
were empty or dismantled. Behind the tarred screens,

Magna a memoir of the enduring human spirit

behind the rusting fly-wire, nothing stirred,
the runways cracked open like an idiot's smile.

The steady salt air
from the open Atlantic rusted bolts,
air hangars, latches, children's toys,
the wooden treaders grave, grey, plumb with rot
From Micoud to L'Anse Paradis
the breakers, like a louder silence, roared.

My mother and most St. Lucians, for that matter most West Indians, had little sway in the war. But as British subjects the colony played its part in the war effort. Six hundred and fifty pounds of St. Lucia's financial contributions were used to purchase two Red Cross ambulances to help in London's war casualty rescue effort. Some of its sons volunteered for the British military and thus joined the theatre of war. Several of them serving as air fighters—including Pilot Officer H.T. Etienne (the first West Indian of African descent to serve as an RAF officer), Henry Dulieu, Desmond Duboulay, and D. Shingleton-Smith—didn't return home; they had made the ultimate sacrifice.

As a preteen at the start of the war and residing deep in the rural interior of the island, my mother would likely have been barely mindful of it as a concrete reality, but, as we shall see later, the war, or rather its aftermath, would have important implications for my mother, her siblings, and her children, and indeed the West Indies civilization.

Besides World War II, in the era of my mother's upbringing and coming of age, St. Lucia experienced several life-changing or epochal calamities, both natural and man-

Wars and Pestilence

made. My mother spoke of the Great Landslide of 1938 when, following a period of heavy rain, the hillside in the vicinity of L'Abbaye, Ravine Poisson, Ravine Chicole, and Ravine Ecrivisse, between the Valleys of Mabouya and Cul-de-Sac, gave way, sweeping and burying everything—people, houses, trees—in its path. She said in the aftermath of the landslide, rescuers found "one arm this side, a leg that side, a head over there." According to some estimates, the landslide, which unfolded in three phases, claimed more than a hundred lives. It was undoubtedly an event that left a lasting impression on my mother and her generation. As a child listening to my mother's account of the landslide, I thought of it as an event of biblical proportions.

A few years before the great 1938 landslide, there were a couple of boat tragedies that though not epoch-changing would have shocked the island and would have definitely reached my mother's ears even though she was still a young child. The first of these disasters occurred on Sunday 24 February 1935, when the M.L. George carrying 115 passengers capsized outside Laborie Bay, drowning 40 people, 37 of whom were from Choiseul, including most members of a church youth group, which caused some people to lament, "All girls of Choiseul have perished." One of the survivors was a pregnant woman who swam more than a mile to shore. Another survivor, of sorts, was on the boat but had just missed the reboarding. When he arrived home, his family's tears of sorrow (thinking he had perished on the boat) turned to tears of joy. Two years later, on Wednesday 17 February 1937, the island mourned 12 more deaths by water when the May Rose capsized outside Soufriere Bay.

When I was growing up, there were a few bus tragedies, usually at night and most times concerning people returning home after attending a dance or other social events that no doubt involved drinking. My parents never failed to use all such incidents as teaching points, lessons of the folly and disastrous consequences of living in iniquity, of indulging in the so-called "good time." So much so that to this day all such accidents bring to mind my parents' admonishment against drinking and feting. When I read of the boat incidents mentioned above, my first reaction was to wonder whether those involved were on a party excursion. The Bible definitely got it right when it admonished: *Train up a child in the way he should go: and when he is old, he will not depart from it.*

I don't recall my mother talking about the 1854 cholera epidemic that caused the death of about 1,500 St. Lucians, or 6 percent of a population of 25,000. It didn't happen in her time, nor in the time of her mother who was born in 1903, nor even in the time of her grandmother, Ma Gill, born 1880, but it would have definitely been in the time of her great grandfather, Pappy Ambroise, who would have related the story to his daughter Sylfide, who would become Ma Gill, who would have related the story to her granddaughter Magna (my mother) and her daughter Marie (Mama Jonah). However, even if adults close to my mother had failed to inform her about the epidemic, since the event had no doubt become part of the island's folk memory, she would likely have been exposed to casual references. So it is conceivable that the cholera epidemic of 1854 was part of my mother's consciousness growing up. After all, it was indeed a catastrophe of biblical proportions. People were

Wars and Pestilence

dying so quickly and in such large numbers that communities resorted to mass graves and quicklime.

Only 20 years removed from slavery, the black population wasn't too keen on marriage. Slavery, after all, was inimical to family life. However, the epidemic put such fear of God in the people that marriages increased more than fivefold. There was such a high demand for matrimony that the Roman Catholic priests, who used to exhort the people to get wedded and stop living in sin, though happy about this unexpected marital turn of events, had great difficulty keeping up. The epidemic-induced high rate of marriages resulted in significant increases in the percentage of legitimate births, such that these births rose from one out of four in 1853, the year before the epidemic, to one out of two in 1862. Such was the impact of the outbreak on the collective consciousness that for generations, undoubtedly down to my mother's generation, the term "*En tan cholera,* in the time of cholera," was a household expression. In terms of its impact on the island, the COVID-19 pandemic (of which my mother was barely conscious, if at all) that caused 409 deaths in St. Lucia over a three-year period (2020-2023) pales in comparison to the 1854 cholera epidemic.

Five months after my mother celebrated her nineteenth birthday, St. Lucia was again visited by a calamity of biblical proportions. On the evening of June 19, 1948, a fire that started at a tailor shop blazed through Castries, gutting three-quarters of the city. Fortunately, unlike the 1938 landslide, the great 1948 Castries fire didn't cause any loss of life, but unfortunately, in terms of property damage, it was an even greater catastrophe, and in terms of social change, it was of much greater import.

Magna a memoir of the enduring human spirit

The fire destroyed **40** blocks of homes and businesses and rendered **809** families or **2293** people homeless. All told, damages amounted to over nine million dollars, inspiring a commentator to characterize the fire as "the greatest calamity to befall a colony of its size and resources in so short a space of time." And on walking through ruins of the fire, eighteen-year-old Derek Walcott and future Nobel Laureate, penned one of his most famous poems, "A City's Death by Fire."

> After that hot gospeller had levelled all but the churched
> sky,
> I wrote the tale by tallow of a city's death by fire;
> Under a candle's eye, that smoked in tears, I
> Wanted to tell, in more than wax, of faiths that were
> snapped like wire.
> All day I walked abroad among the rubbled tales,
> Shocked at each wall that stood on the street like a liar;
> Loud was the bird-rocked sky, and all the clouds were
> bales
> Torn open by looting, and white, in spite of the fire.
> By the smoking sea, where Christ walked, I asked, why
> Should a man wax tears, when his wooden world fails?
> In town, leaves were paper, but the hills were a flock of
> faiths;
> To a boy who walked all day, each leaf was a green
> breath
> Rebuilding a love I thought was dead as nails,
> Blessing the death and the baptism by fire.

Wars and Pestilence

But some good came out of the calamity. The reconstruction effort created a boom in employment and economic activity. Castries gained a modern sewage system, and it expanded into such suburbs as La Clery, Vigie, the Morne, Marchand, and San Soucis, thus reducing the congestion of the city center. And being of no respect of persons, the fire destroyed alike the homes of the rich and poor, the upper class and lower class, leaving all homeless and many penniless, thus forcing them to live several months together in barracks until permanent living arrangements were sorted out, in the process helping to break down class and racial barriers.

My mother must have marveled at the changes the reconstruction of Castries had brought about. The city was almost unrecognizable. It had become one of the most modern of West Indian towns, with contemporary architecture, gridded streets, broad boulevards and thoroughfares, and with less vexing social and class distinctions to boot.

Although my mother didn't mention any other fires, the Great 1948 Fire was by no means the first or last time St. Lucia, and Castries in particular, had been ravaged by fire. About two decades before the 1948 fire and slightly over two years before my mother made her grand entrance into the world, another fire (May 14-15, 1927) that started in the night destroyed 17 blocks of Castries, effectively gutting the business sector. And seven years after the 1948 fire, on June 9, 1955, a Soufriere fire rendered 2000 homeless. Nonetheless, none of these fires come close to matching the sheer catastrophic damage of the Great 1948 Fire.

Magna a memoir of the enduring human spirit

At 51, my mother experienced Hurricane Allen, which she and most St. Lucians would agree was the most destructive hurricane in living memory to visit the island. (I wasn't privileged to bear witness to Allen because at the time I was living in Baton Rouge, Louisiana, where I was attending college). And it seems science would agree with them.

According to the US National Hurricane Center (NHC),[9] originating from the west coast of Africa, Allen was the strongest Atlantic hurricane by wind speed, being the only recorded Atlantic hurricane to achieve sustained winds of 190 mph; it was the second strongest tropical cyclone to hit the Gulf of Mexico; it lasted longer as a Category 5 than all but two other Atlantic hurricanes; and in terms of barometric pressure, it was the fifth most intense Atlantic hurricane in recorded history. It sank fishing boats, uprooted mango, breadfruit, and coconut trees, destroyed homes, roads and bridges, devastated the banana industry, changed the course of rivers, and permanently altered the landscape of certain parts of the island. In the final count, Allen left six dead and US$235 million in collateral damage, which exceeded the gross domestic product (GDP) by 20 percent.

And in the same way that the ruins wrought by the 1948 Castries fire led to the formation of such Castries suburbs as San Souci and La Clery, Allen's destruction of homes in Vieux Fort precipitated the creation of Shantytown (renamed Bruceville) as an extension of the town, and the establishment of Cedar Heights, La Ressource, Contonement, and Derriere Morne as Vieux Fort suburbs.

Although Allen didn't cause much damage to my parents' home in Vieux Fort, it was in the mid-1980s, after the

Wars and Pestilence

hurricane sparked migration to the town's environs, that they relocated to the Vieux Fort outskirt of Upper St. Jude's Highway adjoining Contonement.

Magna in her 70s

CHAPTER ELEVEN

Revolutions and Wedding Bells

ON AUGUST 16, 1949, while Castries was being rebuilt following the Great 1948 Fire, my mother married my father, St. Brice Reynolds. The marriage certificate listed my father as a tailor from Vieux Fort and my mother as a dressmaker from Delomel, East Micoud. They were married at the home of Pastor William Wallace Weithers, with Papa Jonah, Agnes Francis (my mother's third-oldest sister), and Whitney Frederick (no relations) serving as witnesses. My mother was twenty years and seven months old. Although she was the fourth child and four and a half years junior to Francita, the eldest, in keeping with her reputation of being at the forefront, she was the first of her siblings to tie the knot.

How did the matriarch-to-be and the Vieux Fort tailor meet?

Well, my mother said that when she first met my father (I'm assuming they ran into each other in Vieux Fort when my mother came there to sell her goods and buy essentials), he asked, "Do you know who I am?"

Magna a memoir of the enduring human spirit

"Of course," my mother replied. "Aren't you one of those Adventists that does preach in Desruisseaux at the crusade?"

I imagine my father smiling at my mother's sassiness and feeling pleased with himself that the word of God was getting around. At the time, Adventism was just starting to take root in St. Lucia, and my father, a recent convert, would have been among the small group of Adventist pioneers in Vieux Fort and the south of the island. To attend and preach at the Desruisseaux crusade, he would have had to ride his bicycle nightly from Vieux Fort to Desruisseaux and back.

I don't recall my father ever directly relating to us how he first met my mother. But my recollection is that on the pulpit, in one of his sermons—*But seek ye first the kingdom of God, and his righteousness; and all these things shall be added unto you*—my father said that he was always lucky with the ladies. In Vieux Fort, in his tailor shop, plenty of women used to trouble him, but as a recent Seventh-Day Adventist convert and crusader for Christ, he was determined to serve his God. So one night, he fell on his knees and asked God for help choosing his wife. And lo and behold, one night my mother appeared before him in a dream. God had answered his prayers. "Brothers and sisters," my father would exhort his congregation. "It pays to put God first; it pays to put your trust in the Lord."

Duly married, August 1949, while the Americans were decommissioning the Vieux Fort army base and packing up and preparing to leave the island, my mother joined my father in Vieux Fort. Initially, they lived in a house owned by Ma Eber, my father's deceased mother. But according to my mother, ever so often, one or the other of my father's siblings would come and carry away some piece of furniture or another, which they viewed as their mother's property. Finding this indiscretion intolerable, my mother urged my father to "leave the people's house and things for them." So before long, my parents vacated Ma Eber's house and rented their own place.

In 1950, coinciding with my mother giving birth to her first child, named after the prophet Ezekiel, St. Lucia was birthing a revolution[10] on three fronts—political, cultural, and economic. On the political front, there were George Charles, John Compton, and their compatriots fighting for the people's right to a decent living, fighting for decolonization, political empowerment, and self-determination. On the cultural front, there were Harry Simmons, Dunstan St. Omer, the Walcott Brothers, and the other members of the 1950s St. Lucia Arts Guild fighting for the heart and soul of the colony, fighting to decapitate the belief that black meant inferior, to emphatically affirm the notion that St. Lucian culture, St. Lucian way of life, St. Lucian seascape and landscape, were just as deserving as any other of artistic and cultural expression. On the economic front, the banana industry finally took root in St. Lucia and was getting set to dethrone sugar as king, in the process setting off a socioeconomic revolution and further distancing the people from slavery since it was the advent of sugar cane cultivation that had led to the mass importation of Africans as enslaved labor.

I doubt my mother was even aware of the St. Lucia Arts Guild and the cultural renaissance it would spark, for few people outside Castries, or maybe even outside the circles

Magna a memoir of the enduring human spirit

of the Arts Guild, were aware of its existence much less cognizant that a cultural phenomenon was taking place that would serve as the cradle of cultural heroes, Nobel Laureates, and knights. In fact, up till today, few St. Lucians are aware of this phenomenon. I became aware of the exploits of the Arts Guild only upon my return to St. Lucia from my twenty-year North American sojourn at the age of forty when I started delving deeply into St. Lucian literature, art and culture, and was fortunate to attend Dr. Monsignor Patrick Anthony's 2001 Derek Walcott Nobel Laureate lecture on the St. Lucia Arts Guild.

My mother may not have been aware of the St. Lucia Arts Guild, and she wasn't too au courant with popular St. Lucian culture, but she had to have been aware of Dame Marie Selipha Descartes (whose husband was related to her), better known as Sesennè, the island's most famous folk singer, a *Lawòz chantwelle* residing in the Micoud area, who, besides induction into the Caribbean Broadcasting Union Music Hall of Fame, was declared a National Cultural Hero and St. Lucia's Queen of Culture; and whom Derek Walcott celebrated in his poem, "Homecoming," from the collection, *Bounty*.

My country heart, I am not home till Sesenne sings,
a voice with woodsmoke and ground-doves in it, that
cracks
like clay on a road whose tints are the dry season's,
whose cuatros tighten my heartstrings. The shac-shacs
rattle like cicadas under the fur-leaved nettles
of childhood, an old fence at noon, bel-air, quadrille,
la comette, gracious turns, until delight settles.

A voice like rain on a hot road, a smell of cut grass,
its language as small as the cedar's and sweeter than any
wherever I have gone, that makes my right hand Ishmael,
my guide the star-fingered frangipani.

And she definitely would have met, or at the very least
heard of Rameau Poleon (who, by the way, was related to
her husband), also known as *"Papa Kilte,* Father of Culture," the most renowned violinist and folk musician St.
Lucia has produced. He was born the same year as my
mother and passed away in 2024, four years after her death.
He lived in Belle Vue, a mere two miles from Desruisseaux,
my mother's birthplace and upbringing, and an even shorter
distance from our farm in Palmist. With the poem "Thanks,
Rameau," from his 2005 poetry collection, *Phases,* award-
winning St. Lucian poet Modeste Downes immortalized
the celebrated folk musician. The third verse of his poem
confesses,

> I have stood in sacramental awe
> Imbibing each stanza of fluid note
> That flowed like magic from your vyolon's lips;
> You are an alphabet of mystique
> Each time I have watched you play:
> Hat askew, fingers walking the body
> Of the thing you necked like a lover,
> Your feet light, tap dancing on the spot.

My mother never concerned herself much with politics
(things outside her control) and sports and art (things she
probably perceived as of little practical value or holding no

place in God's Kingdom). She kept her eyes on the ball of feeding, clothing, housing, educating her children, and keeping them on the straight and narrow path. She kept her focus on things within her control, on variables she could manipulate and bend to her will. But she definitely would have caught wind of the heroics of George Charles, his labor strike activities, and, like the rest of the island, she would have rejoiced at the attainment of the right to vote regardless of gender, wealth or class.

My mother, no doubt, would have also heard of the heroics of John Compton, particularly his involvement in the 1957 sugar strike when he visited the Dennery sugar factory to speak to the owner and manager, Denis Barnard, about better wages and working conditions for workers, only to face the barrel of his gun. It was a moment that held the masses spellbound, after which Compton was hailed the hero who had entered the citadel, the inner cave of the plantocracy, the enemy of the people, and insisted on the people's right to dignity and decent living, and began the dismantling of the edifice of the plantation system that was responsible for the people's enslavement, servitude and deprivation.

Before long (1964), Compton would displace George Charles as the head of government and lead St. Lucia into statehood to become the first and only premier of St. Lucia. He and his United Workers Party would hold the reins of power for 30 years (1964-1996) of almost unbroken rule, in the process leading the country into independence; and Compton, hailed by many as the father of the nation and by some the St. Lucia man of the century, served as the first and to date the longest standing prime minister (1979, 1982-1996, 2006-2007) of St. Lucia.

Revolutions and Wedding Bells

In any event, my father was an avid follower of politics, West Indies cricket, and world news (especially the BBC World News report), and he didn't miss an opportunity for an engaging conversation. And besides, his brother Jean Reynolds, a UK-educated lawyer, had contested the general elections of 1964 as an independent candidate and again in 1969 and 1974 as a St. Lucia Labor Party (SLP) candidate. I remember my father helping with his campaign. My uncle lost miserably in these elections. So much so that on the eve of yet another election, he threatened that this time around if he were to lose the elections, he would throw himself in the sea, *Juboom!* Of course, he lost the election, but I'm not sure that he carried out his threat. However, after that his name changed to *Juboom*. So even if my mother weren't too keen on politics and world news, my father would have filled her in on the happenings of the day.

My uncle never won an election, indeed he kept losing miserably, but it seems he was something of a political cult hero. A retired secondary school teacher recalls Jean Reynolds' political campaign when he was vying for the Dennery North seat.

As children, we always enjoyed the political campaigns, all parts of it, because the slogans were decent and catchy. I recalled Jean Reynolds' slogan; it went something like this: *Jean-ou sé jean-ou; tout moun bouzwen an jean. Jean Reynolds sé jean; bay Jean Reynolds voté-la.* (Your friend is your friend; everyone needs a friend. Jean Reynolds is your friend; give Jean Reynolds the vote). We all would join with him and kept repeating this

Magna a memoir of the enduring human spirit

slogan throughout the campaign. And we all enjoyed saying the name Jean Reynolds.

Both my parents were partial to John Compton. My father used to express concern that Compton would be assassinated and that if he were Compton, he would finish with politics. In contrast, he always complained about Prime Minister (1997-2006, 2011- 2016) Kenny Anthony piling up national debt and warned that if the prime minister weren't careful, he would bankrupt the country. My mother also complained about Dr. Kenny Anthony. She would say, "*Sa ki wivé misyé sala, i toujou anwajé?* What's wrong with this man? He is always in a rage?" But when it came to Prime Minister (2007-2011) Stephenson King of the United Workers Party, she would say, "*Sa sé an bèl misye, bon mannyè.* He is a handsome man with nice ways."

My parents' disposition toward Kenny Anthony was a bit perplexing, for he was credited with bringing about a kinder and gentler country. More than most other heads of government, he safeguarded workers' rights; catered to the most vulnerable citizens with low-income housing, ambitious employment programs, and social safety nets; promoted equitable access to services and opportunities; professionalized the civil service; augmented the country's sports, health, cultural and educational assets; and introduced universal secondary school education from which my parents' grandchildren directly benefited.

Also, my mother definitely would have heard of George Odlum and Peter Josie, not only because they were perhaps regarded as St. Lucia's most formidable and firebrand political duo but also because they presided over and were the

Revolutions and Wedding Bells

main instigators or architects of what many considered St. Lucia's most tumultuous and perilous political epoch.[11] With their talk of Black Power, socialism, communism, revolutions, taking from the haves to give to the have-nots, land reform and nationalization, and overthrowing the Compton United Workers Party (UWP) government and grabbing hold of power by any means necessary, including violence, they struck fear in the hearts of many St. Lucians and was one of the reasons my father was fearful that Compton would be assassinated.

Yet many other St. Lucians, the youth especially, viewed the duo as liberators, a foil to Compton's (perceived) dictatorship or autocratic style of governance. Possessing an acute intellect, great charisma, and spellbinding oratory prowess, George Odlum was revered and praised for his political and economic empowerment of the masses, for raising political consciousness, and for helping to rid St. Lucians of their self-contempt.

In his poem, "The Passing of a Great Man" (from the collection, *Phases*), Modeste Downes echoed the sentiments of many St. Lucians on the death of George Odlum.

Like a mighty oak
in time's forested valley,
you came crashing down
with a pre-empting thud;
And the smaller oaks around you
twirled and whimpered
at your falling,
While bigger, more towering oaks,

In fraternal sincerity
or impious ostentations,
Bowed solemnly
and sang sweet hosannahs
to your name
that detonated like a cannon.

.

.

.

In parting, you taught too,
That truth is truth,
though we spite the carrier
or scorn the parchment on which it is inscribed;
And that the forest
that grew that once mighty oak,
Is no more incapable now,
of producing other oaks
to replace felled ones;
That 'the struggle' that took your life
must not die with your passing;
And that, finally
the forest be sheltered
by a canopy of love,
that all may grow unwanting,
Bearing fruit that is pleasing,
till we face the Eternal Logger.

Notwithstanding all that the George Odlum-Peter Josie
duo brought to the picture, I can understand why they never
would have stood a chance with my parents. First, in my
parents' strict Seventh-Day Adventist eyes, communism was

Revolutions and Wedding Bells

synonymous with atheism and the disbanding of Christianity. Second, for people whose lives personify hard work and lifting oneself by one's bootstraps, the notion of taking from the haves ("the hardworking") to give to the have-nots ("the lazy") was a definite no-no. Third, the threat of a coup d'état and its inherent violence and unlawfulness could not sit well with Adventists intent on keeping their children on the straight and narrow path and who placed great stock in being law-abiding citizens and keeping the Ten Commandments.

Nonetheless, in 1979 the duo got their chance to rule when their party, the St. Lucia Labour Party, got into power not by coup d'état but by a 12 to 5 electoral victory.

I don't know which party my mother voted for or if she voted at all, but this was the first general election in which I was eligible to vote, and to date, it has been my most agonizing voting decision. The St. Lucia Labor Party of that period was by far the most educated and qualified political party in the history of the island, so as a twenty-year-old with higher-education aspirations and wanting the best for my country, it should have been my great pleasure to vote for the SLP, but my conscience dictated that I vote for the UWP; I couldn't bring myself to vote for a party that was advocating violence as a means of getting into power, after all I'm a product of my parents, my upbringing. Nonetheless, the SLP victory brought me great relief. The country had escaped the bloodshed that may have accompanied an SLP defeat, and the party with the most to offer the country had prevailed.

But sadly, the SLP's aspirations and intentions were never fulfilled because an internal power struggle between

Prime Minister Allan Louisy and Deputy Prime Minister George Odlum led to the dissolution of the government in mid-term, and, in the general elections that followed, John Compton and his United Workers Party returned to power by a 14 to 3 majority, and would hold on to power for another 15 years or three election cycles.

MY MOTHER MAY NOT HAVE PAID much attention to politics and culture and wasn't much of a player on the political and cultural revolutionary front, but when it came to the banana industry and the socioeconomic revolution it spawned, she and her husband and their children were in the thick of it. Upon my father's return to St. Lucia in the early sixties, following his five-year stint in the UK, besides re-establishing his tailor shop, one of his first major investments was the purchase of four acres of farmland, albeit with the coaxing of my mother and his lawyer/politician brother Jean Reynolds, for my father was very cautious and risk-averse, and who could blame him? With so many children to feed, there wasn't much room for error.

The farm was in Palmist, between Grace and Belle Vue in Vieux Fort North. The Vieux Fort River, at a more youthful stage, ran alongside the land. It was a fertile, well-watered land of black loam soil traversed by a *wavin* or two that emptied into the river. When you are on the land, you get the impression that you are in the deep heights. Beyond the river, the land rises into the heavens to the hills of Belle Vue. In the opposite direction, on the other boundary, the land rises sharply to give rise to Grace.

On this land, indulging his love of farming and nature, my father would paint his Sistine Chapel. But more impor-

Revolutions and Wedding Bells

tantly, with the banana industry in full swing, the land would become a Mecca of banana production and yield a bountiful supply of fruits, cashew nuts, breadfruits, breadnuts, and ground provisions. My parents may not have always been able to put meat on our plates, but with the farm we always had an abundance of fruits and vegetables, so we never went hungry. The proceeds from bananas helped my parents feed, clothe and educate us; enabled my father to expand into trucking, transporting passengers and bananas; and in general raise the family's standard of living. Our home expanded from a one-bedroom to a three-bedroom house, then we added a walled kitchen and bath, and we graduated from an outdoor latrine to a flush toilet. Our economic survival came to rest on four main pillars—tailoring, banana cultivation, beekeeping, and trucking.

Perhaps what I associated most with the economic progress of my family was the acquisition of a telephone in my teenage years. I don't know why to me it signified advancement more than the other things the family had acquired, except maybe at the time I saw it as a luxury item that wasn't directly linked to our material well-being.

It was a red rotary-dial desk phone, placed in the same corner of the living room that my father's precious tabletop radio set occupied, the radio that he brought from London in the early 60s, on which he listened to the BBC World News and play-by-play West Indies cricket commentary; cricket, that once sacred and beloved sport that symbolized the very essence of the West Indies civilization or the best of what the West Indies could be.

The telephone, like the radio, was no plaything. The corner they occupied was sacred, like an altar to knowledge, culture, communications, and progress. No other part of the house epitomized my father more than this corner. Although he was in a constant bread-and-butter struggle to feed, clothe, and educate his family, he spent daily time in that corner, catching up with the outside world and following West Indies cricket. Knowing we took sneak listening to cricket even on the Sabbath, behind my mother's back my otherwise strict Seventh-Day Adventist father would ask us for score updates when he could no longer withstand the suspense.

In much the same way my family was among the first in Vieux Fort (or at the very least in my neighborhood) to own a radio, a refrigerator, and a vehicle, it was one of the early adopters of the telephone, which became another possession that signified that my parents were progressive and ahead of their time, and that made Vieux Fortians believe we were rich, even though I didn't know any other family that worked as hard as we did, which used to make me wonder if we were so rich, how come we were working so hard?

Now, when I survey the socioeconomic landscape of Vieux Fort, I realize that my family wasn't all that unique, for many of the people who could be regarded as progressive and ahead of their time were those who, like my parents, had spent time abroad—alas the benefits of travel and migration. But then we have the chicken and egg situation, for it turns out it is usually the most ambitious people, those who would have made headway even if they had stayed put, who are likely to migrate. So the chicken and egg question is, was it living abroad that made people like my parents progressive, or was it their inherent progressive and ambitious nature that caused them to choose (self-select themselves for) migration in the first place? Statisticians and economists have a term for this phenomenon—self-selectivity or self-selection bias.

As expected, the telephone served not just the family. Our neighbors and parents' friends came to make and sometimes receive calls, as did my mother's sisters, nieces, and nephews from the countryside, who sometimes made the seven-mile bus trip just to make or receive overseas calls. If I remember correctly, my ever-enterprising and proactive mother even added telecom service as yet another one of her income-generating enterprises.

ALL THIS PROGRESS and seeming affluence were great, but there was a catch. We, the children, became part of my parents' labor force. And to make matters worse, we had to hike about a mile downhill from the motorable road, then cross the river to get to the farm. My father harvested bananas every two weeks, which meant that we skipped a whole day of school every other week to engage in a banana-carrying odyssey. On those days, all day we carried load after load of bananas on our heads across the river, sometimes raging (especially during the rainy season), uphill along the slippery footpath to the road. We would leave home before dawn and sometimes return home after midnight. I think I was about seven when I started carrying bananas, and my younger brother started even younger than that. Above, I hinted at the hard life my mother and her siblings endured when they were growing up, but I must say that we, her children, didn't have it too easy either.

Bananas were such a socioeconomic boon that green gold, as it was dubbed, was a fitting name for the crop. As

Magna a memoir of the enduring human spirit

banana cultivation spread throughout the island, the network of motorable roads extended into the deep interior; pipe water, electricity, primary schools, and health centers spread to such rural hamlets as Desruisseaux, Belle Vue, and beyond. The *ajupas* and straw huts gave way to multiple-room lumber and wall houses; teachers, lawyers, tradesmen, all got into the act of cultivating bananas. Farmers were able to send their children to secondary schools and universities, and with their trucks displaying FAR (short for farmer) license plates, farmers gave the impression that they were ruling the world.

Sugarcane cultivation was capital-intensive and entailed a once-a-year crop and cash inflow. It was economically feasible only on large expanses of easily accessible land and thus was concentrated in the hands of a few centralized estates and sugar factories. In contrast, banana cultivation was suitable for small plots of land and a greater variety of terrain. All a farmer needed to secure a piece of the action was a machete, a fork or a pickaxe, and a parcel of land of any size. Understandably, banana cultivation mushroomed across the island, where every banana farmer, no matter how small their enterprise, was an individual business decision-maker with banana proceeds flowing into his pocket (or, in the case of women, the space between their breasts) weekly or biweekly. Therefore, compared to sugarcane, bananas fostered economic empowerment, geographically balanced economic prosperity, and a more egalitarian distribution of wealth, and thus helped in the nurturing of the island's democracy.

Indeed, farmers became such a powerful voting bloc with the ability to swing general elections that to ignore their concerns and demands was to commit political suicide. However, the downside of this reality for the farmers was that the politicians took to pandering for their votes and using institutions like the St. Lucia Banana Growers Association (SLBGA), established to advance the banana industry, as vehicles for getting elected.

Alas, green gold wasn't all it cracked up to be. It came with some serious unintended consequences. Its unparalleled success undermined agricultural and economic diversification and was tantamount to replacing one mono-cultural economic system—sugar—with another—bananas. Its suitability to most terrain meant that farmers went banana crazy. They indiscriminately cut down the forest on steep slopes to plant bananas even in the water catchment areas, which led to the lowering of the island's water table, the drying up of its rivers and *wavins*, as well as massive erosion, the silting and clogging of its rivers, and the destruction of its mangrove forests and coastline ecosystem.

But the environmental degradation probably went deeper than that because the application of banana chemicals—fertilizer, herbicides, nematicides—may have caused untold health problems, as hinted by the decimation of the slow-moving toads, the size of breadfruits, that once inhabited the farm like it was their kingdom, the near disappearance of fish and crawfish in our rivers, and the dearth of soil microorganisms. Some blame the farm chemicals and banana cultivation practices for the disappearance of some of the wild plants—*agouman, zeb épina, sijean, banja, bawé bef, zeb a koues, zeb aye*—that served as sources of food for my mother's generation.

Magna a memoir of the enduring human spirit

The particular case of the French Antilles of Martinique and Guadeloupe is telling. These twin islands continued to use chlordecone to protect banana plants against root borers right up to 1993, even though the US stopped producing Kepone (chlordecone's marketed name) since 1975 when its harmful effects became known. Today, chlordecone, which is linked to a greater incidence of prostate cancer in the twin islands and which scientists suspect increases the risk of premature births and adverse brain development in children, is found in the blood of over 90 percent of the adult population of these two islands, and about half of their agricultural lands are contaminated with this chemical.[12] I'm sure my mother would have been appalled to discover that the crop that had contributed so much to her family's financial well-being and to her country's material progress had come with so many bads.

Like most St. Lucian banana farmers, my father applied the herbicide Gramoxone to his fields. He mixed the Gramoxone with water in a large drum, from which he filled the herbicide spray machine. As children, we innocently played in the cool, enticing Gramoxone mixture. Even today, I wonder how the chemical has affected our health.

IN ALL THE FAMILY'S SURVIVAL ACTIVITIES, my mother was not only in the thick of it, but in some instances she was the initiator. I never witnessed her carrying bananas, but she was the first to be up and about on banana day, gathering all the cooking supplies and utensils. On the farm, she would cook the meals on pit fires or coal pots and ensure everyone was well fortified for the work ahead. The following day, she was up before daybreak to prepare

Revolutions and Wedding Bells

breakfast and ensure everyone, no matter how tired, sleepy, or sore, made their way to school.

On Sundays, she accompanied us to the farm to gather the family's weekly supply of fruits and ground provisions such as yams, dasheen, tania, cush-cush, breadnut, breadfruit, bananas, plantain, *makabou*, plums, golden apples, oranges, grapefruit. Yet I don't think my mother enjoyed the heights and being on the farm all that much, at least not like my father. She was all about utility, extracting all that was available, leaving nothing to waste or to thieves or the birds, mongoose, rats, and toads. When we left the farm on Sundays, any thief, human or otherwise, lying in wait would have been greatly disappointed.

With our father, the story was completely different. He left us to our own devices and went about his farm as if greeting every plant, every living creature by name, and day-dreaming of the size of next week's banana harvest. We would hurriedly collect the produce and fruits to get home early to play ball or go to a football match. Our efforts were not designed to gather all that was available but to collect just enough for our mother to see we had made a credible effort and thus avoid her tongue-lashing.

To be in my mother's world was to be in a beehive of activity. It was no place for the lazy. Always something to do, always something doing. Up to my early childhood, my mother baked bread to sell and operated a mom-and-pop store. Later, she baked every Friday, but just for the family and in preparation for the Saturday Sabbath. Mid-week, the boys went into the bush to collect and carry home dry wood to fuel the oven. Fridays were particularly hectic: the house and yard were swept clean, all meals for the evening and the following day were prepared, Sabbath clothes well ironed, and shoes polished to a shine. But Sabbath eating was good. Plenty of homemade juice and my mother's bread, cake, fried fish, and roasted breadfruit and sweet potato.

Regarding honey production, my father maintained the hives and, with our help, harvested the honey. But once the honeycomb got home, my mother took over because at home my father had to switch his attention to tailoring, constructing hives, vehicle maintenance, transporting people and bananas, or preparing sermons. She and we children manually squeezed the honey from the comb, then she strained the honey and purified it by placing it over a slow heat, during which the impurities rose to the surface and thus easily scooped out from the golden-brown honey. Then she stored the honey in five-gallon containers for wholesale and export markets and quart-size bottles for the retail market, which were sold from home. Later, when my father bought a drum-like honey extraction machine that worked by centrifugal force, we got a break in that the honeycomb-squeezing step was eliminated.

Thanks to the farm, the family produced copra two to three times a year. The dry coconuts that had fallen from the trees were assembled, and those still on the trees were picked either by long gullets or by hand, which meant climbing the trees. Then the nuts were de-husked, the kernel split in half, the water discarded, and the kernels carried in sacs on our heads to the road. Once the kernels reached home, my mother took over. She supervised the placing of the kernels on the galvanized roof for drying into copra, the removal of the shells from the copra, and the ramming of the copra into sacs for transporting to the coconut factory in Soufriere. Later, after my father bought an estate in the Grace area, which, though not as fertile as the first estate, was next to the road, he built a copra kiln right on the farm; thus we didn't have to carry the kernels home for drying on the roof.

As if the farm wasn't enough land and didn't generate enough work, my mother turned her yard into a kitchen garden. No. She turned her yard into a second farm. It mattered little that the yard was mostly stones and solid rock with very little topsoil. *Since when has my mother let anything stop her?* And what did she have us for? Who else but her children would collect and carry home the soil, manure and seaweed that would enable her to turn her yard of rocks into a basket of sweet potato, corn, lettuce, carrot, peanuts, cucumber, pumpkin, watermelon, celery, and the list goes on.

She was practicing organic farming long before it came into vogue. The only thing she didn't bargain for was that her garden would be a Mecca for toads. But for this she also had a solution. When they got in her way, she had us pour salt on them (apparently, my mother didn't buy into the notion of live and let live), which was a kind of torture for me because, like her, I too was afraid of frogs, yet I had to get close to them to pour the salt.

My mother's industriousness didn't stop at farming, gardening, baking, and honey processing. At some point, the family bought a fridge and a deep freezer. So in addition to storing the neighbors' fish and meat in the deep freezer for fee, my mother sold ice and ventured into the business of selling frozen icicles with her children serving as icicle hawkers. She also made ice lollies, coconut pralines, and guava, gooseberry, and golden apple jams to sell. To avoid waste and bring in additional income, she sold the farm's surplus of fruits, bananas, and ground provisions from home. My mother's home was a nonstop tailor shop (for this, my father was to blame, not her), food processing plant, and retail outlet. God may have given my mother to my father in a dream; if so, He would have been hard-pressed to find him a better and more willing helpmate.

My mother's bountifulness carried over to establishing her clan, her most precious, the names of whom, as she lay dying, she kept repeating like a mantra. Within the first decade of her marriage, she gave birth to seven of her nine children. She gave birth to Ezekiel, her firstborn, in 1950, followed by Ezildra, her first daughter, in 1951; then Margareta, her third child and second daughter, in 1952; then McEachrane, her fourth child and second son, in 1954, followed by her third son, McElryn, in 1955; and then her sixth child and third and last daughter, Magdalina, in 1957.

Then it was my turn, the seventh child, born prematurely in 1958, to be named Anderson after my father's London doctor. I guess this was his way of tricking the universe into ensuring that I became a doctor. It had always been his life-long dream for one of his children to be a medical doctor. Yet he wasn't around to welcome my birth. By then he had migrated to the UK. I am the only one of my father's children whose birth he wasn't there to welcome.

My father got double what he had wished, but not really. Although two of his children are doctors (and he had attended both their graduations as they received their doctor of philosophy degrees), they are doctors of economics, not doctors of medicine. His dream of a physician was fulfilled through his granddaughter, my youngest sister's daughter, but sadly he exited this life long before she obtained her medical degree. Still, I imagine he would have taken comfort in knowing that as a medical doctor his granddaughter had been part of his daughter Zel's medical support team caring for his wife as she lay dying.

I was followed in 1960 by my brother, Prosper, born not in St. Lucia but in London because my mother had left her seven children in the care of her father and younger sisters to join my father in England. Hubert, the last child, came along in 1968, eight years after the brother before him, when we thought my mother had long stopped making children. All along, I never noticed that my mother was with child. You see, because of a medical condition, she appeared permanently pregnant. That day when my father came to the Plain View School to pick us up, he said, "Mama make another Prosper," which to me meant that I had a baby brother. This was when I first realized my mother had been with child.

I suspect my father named all his children. I wonder whether he had given as much importance or invested as much meaning in the naming of his children as did his African forebears. Nevertheless, I'm baffled by some of the names. Obviously, Ezekiel, my eldest brother, was named after the Old Testament prophet, and maybe my youngest sister, Magdalina, was named after Mary Magdalene. My father revealed that he named me after his doctor in England, he named my brother born in England Prosper to signify or ensure his prosperity, and he named my youngest brother Hubert after his father, Hubert Reynolds.

An internet search revealed that Margaretta, the name of my second eldest sister, is a plant genus in the family of Apocynaceae, and as a Persian baby name it means child of light, while in Greek it means pearl. Of course, I don't know (but doubt) that my father was aware of (or acted on) this information when naming my sister. The other names—Ezildra, McEachrane, and McElryn—sound like heavy Irish or Scottish names, yet I'm not aware that my father had much contact with Irish or Scots before his stay in the UK. I can't help but wonder what significance these names held for him.

Names notwithstanding, my mother's nine children were her most precious.

CHAPTER TWELVE

London Calling

DURING ITS POST-WORLD WAR II REBUILDING efforts and economic boom, war-torn Britain encountered crippling labor shortages that, despite its racial prejudices, forced it to open its doors to immigration from the Commonwealth. On the other hand, faced with extreme poverty, debilitating unemployment, deplorable living conditions, landlessness, glaring class and racial divisions, and government neglect, the West Indian masses must have viewed the opening of UK borders as a godsend. From the late forties to early sixties, they flocked to England by shiploads, going down in history as the "Windrush Generation," in reference to the HMT Empire Windrush,[13] one of the early vessels that brought the West Indians to their new home.

During the 1956 -1960 five-year period, no less than 5250 St. Lucians migrated to London, representing roughly 6 percent of an average population of 90 thousand. My father joined this mass UK migration in early 1958, leaving behind my mother and six children, with one on the way (me).

My mother had a difficult time coping with my father's absence. Ezildra, my eldest sister, said that in our father's absence my mother had something akin to a nervous breakdown. She would claw at the house's partitions, forcing one of the neighbors to come and calm her down.

Employment-wise, London was working well for my father. He had found work in a tailor shop and was progressing so rapidly and so smoothly that the owner was predicting that before long West Indians like my father would take over London. But on the social and family side, he wasn't faring too well. He said that in my mother's absence he was under great temptation. The women saw him as a catch and wouldn't leave him alone. Yet he wanted to remain true to his God and his wife.

Other West Indian single men in London had a different problem. So many of them had migrated to the UK that there was an acute shortage of West Indian women to wed, so many had to import their wives by sending boat fares back home for their families to send them brides. The prospects of leaving behind the then depressive social and economic life of the West Indies for the rich, exciting life London promised proved more than enough incentive for the young women to accept the free passage to London and betrothal to someone they hadn't met. Some of these newly arrived young women were marrying men much older than what was once considered acceptable, and some teachers, nurses, and office workers were marrying one-time laborers and agricultural workers they'd never have wedded back home, considering the men's much lower social status. Unsurprisingly, a few of the brides-to-be never fulfilled their promise of marriage, choosing instead to escape and hide from their intended husbands upon arrival in London.

With the separation causing my mother to suffer nervous breakdowns and my father to endure loneliness and temptations of the flesh, husband and wife must have felt compelled to reunite in London. This way, with both of them working, it would take less time to meet their financial goals and return home. Besides, they weren't doing anything outside of the ordinary. At the time, it was customary for parents to leave their children in the care of relatives to enable them to migrate in search of a better life for their family or to send their children to live with relatives in another part of the island to gain easier access to education or even to enjoy a better standard of living.

My mother left for England to join my father in 1959 at the age of twenty-nine, leaving her seven children in the care of her father and one or more of her younger sisters.

West Indians like my parents migrated to England en masse, but the UK was by no means a bed of roses. Far from it. They found an England of "No French, No Irish, No Dogs, and No Blacks," where management, skilled labor, office positions, and other more appealing and better-paying occupations were reserved for Whites, while they were mostly relegated to low-paying factory and minimum wage jobs. It wasn't uncommon for the employment office to send them to fill skilled job vacancies only to arrive on-site and, being of the wrong color, be told the vacancy had been filled.

As a direct consequence of the war, London faced severe housing shortages, and from the West Indians' point of view the housing shortage was even more acute because some racist landlords refused outright even to consider renting to them.

Magna a memoir of the enduring human spirit

Still, for many West Indians, especially the frugal ones, this was a leg up. At the very least they could find jobs, something as scarce at home as gold; and in between jobs they could collect welfare, something unheard of where they were from. To save on rent and to accommodate themselves to the housing shortage, real or imposed, they bunched up in hostels, several of them sleeping on the same bed. Such living arrangements may have been unacceptable to the English, but for the West Indians these hostel rooms were probably the same size or larger than the wooden shacks in which they were raised, and the beds that three or four of them shared beat out any day the six to thirteen of them as children sleeping on the floor on *kabann* where they were prey to mice, cockroaches, centipedes, and sometimes even toads, my nemesis. And the jobs may have been low-paying, menial, arduous and unpleasant by UK standards, but they may have seemed like child's play for people who, growing up, had to walk miles across rivers, hills and valleys to get to school; who had no choice but to work in the tropical heat in rat and snake-infested cane fields, or who had to endure the arduous, all-day task of carrying on their heads multiple bunches of bananas from farm to motorable roads.

In London, my parents and one of my mother's younger sisters shared a hostel room where the three slept on the same bed. My mother found work on the assembly line at a garment factory, stitching buttons onto suits.

I can well imagine the culture shock London presented to my mother. Here she was, from a tiny, backward island (even by West Indian standards) of only 90 thousand souls, raised in a vale in a rural hamlet without electricity, running water, and indoor plumbing. An island with so few motor vehicles that teenage boys knew every single vehicle in their area by their number plates and the sound of their engines. The tallest buildings she had laid eyes on were no more than three stories high. Then suddenly, she finds herself in a city of over eight million people, of palaces, trains, underground tunnels, and red double-decker buses; of streets with no end, of throngs of people everywhere.

The culture shock was so intense, and London made such a lasting impression on my mother that for the rest of her life she continued talking about the city as if she had just returned from there a day ago. Even as she lay dying, she was extolling the superiority of the UK medical and hospital system over that of St. Lucia. Interestingly, my mother's talk of the UK wasn't about things—palaces, waterways, bridges, monuments—but about people, her interactions with coworkers and employers, how she stood up for herself against discrimination on the job, how she secured or demanded the pay she deserved, how she made herself so indispensable on the job that she was able to keep it even though initially her employer wanted to get rid of her because as an Adventist she refused to work on Saturdays.

I have forgotten the details of most of my mother's London stories. But two stand out in my mind, and both have to do with money.

My mother said she received the winning pool numbers in a dream. But since, as an Adventist, she doesn't gamble, she gave the numbers to a Ghanaian co-worker. The following week, when she asked about the whereabouts of the coworker, she was informed that her colleague had won the

Magna a memoir of the enduring human spirit

pools, big time, and returned to Ghana. As a child, I was a bit taken aback that my mother showed no signs of regret for not playing the pools herself or vexation at the ungratefulness of the co-worker who hadn't even bothered to inform her of the good news, much less share the bounty with her. I guess my mother's disposition attested to her steadfastness in her religion and her unwillingness to take shortcuts in life.

In the second story, my mother said that she found a bag full of money on the compound of her workplace, which she handed over to the establishment. It turned out there was a bank robbery during the winter, and upon police pursuit the robbers apparently flung the bag over the wall of the compound. Snow must have fallen, covering up the bag, until my mother found it as Spring was coming on and the snow was thawing. Her coworkers chided her, saying in effect, *How could you be so stupid? Do you intend to slave for the British for the rest of your life?* But my mother was unperturbed. She wasn't interested in what didn't belong to her. She lived the example of what she tried to inculcate in her children—there is no free lunch; work is the only path to success.

Nonetheless, when my mother was relating these stories, I used to think, *damn, we had an opportunity to be rich twice over, but she didn't take it.* On top of that, I remembered my father saying that if he had stayed in England longer, he would have gotten rich. I wondered why he hadn't stayed and sent for us. I suspected it would have been too burdensome raising eight children in this crowded, housing-shortage city, and he probably didn't want to raise his children as second-class citizens. Of

London Calling

course, this was just my guess; my father never explained, and I never thought of asking.

CULTURE SHOCK NOTWITHSTANDING, given how much and how long my mother dwelt on the UK, you would think she had spent decades there. But she was only there for at most two years, and for most of that time she had been either pregnant or caring for her baby, her eighth child. Her sojourn in England was cut short just when she had probably gotten over the culture shock of London and was acclimatizing to the weather and big city life. Reports were coming in that the children she left behind were being ill-treated. The older ones were misbehaving and going astray. And the younger ones were sickly and malnourished and suffered from withdrawal symptoms; in brief, they had *chagwen manman-yo*, meaning their mother's absence had driven them into a state of depression and sadness. So my mother had little choice but to return home to look after her children.

Apparently, it was a very unwelcome move. My mother's older sisters said she was miserable about her premature departure from London. She arrived home full of frustration and vexation. One of her sisters said that upon visiting my mother, she witnessed her flinging one child there and another over there, forcing her to conclude that if it's like that she had to treat her children, then it's best she never had any.

How accurate is this report? I don't know. Understandably, my mother would have been frustrated about having to return home so soon. But wouldn't she have had a longing to see her children? Wouldn't she be worried about

Magna a memoir of the enduring human spirit

their welfare? Some years ago, one of my brothers had cautioned me. He said that I had to take what the aunts said about our mother with a grain of salt because there was always rivalry amongst siblings. Knowing how my mother and her siblings grew up and their likely intense rivalry, I think my brother's caution was justified.

Sometimes, during my mother's illness, I would sit at her bedside, keeping her company even though she might be asleep, listening to the sound of her breathing and watching her chest move in rhythm with her breathing. At such times, as she lay bedridden with nothing but time on her hands, I would wonder what she was thinking; was she reflecting on her life? She had spoken so much about London; was she now reflecting on her decision to join my father in England? Did she have any regrets? In hindsight, would she have done it again? After all, this may well have been one of the biggest decisions of her life, one of the most momentous from her children's point of view, because the separation and neglect and abuse they suffered left, I surmise, a lasting impact on their personalities and on who they became.

I was about 12 months old when my mother departed, so the mother-child bond that forms during the first three and a half years of a child's life was aborted, never to be completed, never to be made whole, because the window of opportunity had closed for good. The separation spiraled me into a state of *chagwen* (depression and sadness) and resulted in a damaged psyche and maladjusted behavior that has conditioned my life. It was said that after my mother left, I cried incessantly, I became underweight and sickly, I was shitting on me still standing up, and I went around asking women if they were my mother. When my mother returned, it was clear I didn't yet accept her as my mother because I was still going around asking other women if they were my mother.

I was the youngest of the children my mother left behind, and so was probably the most affected by her absence. I grew up knowing something wasn't quite right with me and the family, and I reasoned that my mother's departure to England must have played a big part in it. My accosting of my parents when I was thirteen years old to present a theory explaining the behavior of each of my siblings was a reflection of my feeling that something was amiss with the family and an attempt to come to terms with it.

However, my mother was averse to revisiting this the most telling episode of my life and providing answers to my when, why, and how. Her unwillingness to discuss the topic filled me with angst and frustration and left me with the task of solving the biggest riddle of my life all by myself. Accordingly, I spent all my childhood and most of my early adulthood trying to decipher what was wrong with me and why I wasn't the person I thought I was meant to be.

Eventually, as a mature adult, I looked up what psychiatrists had to say about the symptoms and consequences of mother-infant separations. It turned out that they had a definite diagnosis and name that came close to what I had endured. Can you imagine my surprise, shock, even, along with a sprinkling of amusement (a wry smile of disbelief) that I had spent all those years trying to unravel my life's mystery while all along behavioral scientists could have not only described what exactly was wrong with me but given me its actual name?

According to psychiatrists, when the bond between an infant and her primary caregiver is disrupted or not securely developed, often as a result of abuse, neglect, or separation from the primary caregiver, the infant is prone to develop attachment disorders, one of which is called reactive attachment disorder (RAD).

The Diagnostic and Statistical Manual, 5th Edition, classifies reactive attachment disorder as a trauma and stressor-related condition of early childhood caused by social neglect or maltreatment. Affected children have difficulty forming emotional attachments to others, show a decreased ability to experience positive emotion, cannot seek or accept physical or emotional closeness, and may react violently when held, cuddled, or comforted. Behaviorally, affected children are unpredictable, difficult to console, and difficult to discipline. Moods fluctuate erratically, and children may seem to live in a "flight, fight, or freeze" mode. Most have a strong desire to control their environment and make their own decisions. Spontaneous changes in the child's routine, attempts to discipline the child, or even unsolicited invitations of comfort may elicit rage, violence, or self-injurious behavior. In the classroom, these challenges inhibit the acquisition of core academic skills and lead to rejection from teachers and peers alike. As they approach adolescence and adulthood, socially neglected children are more likely than their neuro-typical peers to engage in high-risk sexual behavior, substance abuse, involvement with the legal system, and experience incarceration. [14,15]

It seems that such infant trauma causes not just maladjusted behavior but also permanent physiological damage.

This is what happens inside children when they are forcibly separated from their parents.

Their heart rate goes up. Their body releases a flood of stress hormones such as cortisol and adrenaline. Those stress hormones can start killing off dendrites—the little branches in brain cells that transmit messages. In time, the stress can start killing off neurons and—especially in young children—wreaking dramatic and long-term damage, both psychologically and to the physical structure of the brain.

Those (children at Romanian orphanages) separated from their parents at a young age had much less white matter, which is largely made up of fibers that transmit information throughout the brain, as well as much less gray matter, which contains the brain-cell bodies that process information and solve problems...The children, who had been separated from their parents in their first two years of life, scored significantly lower on IQ tests later in life...What alarmed the researchers most was the duration of the damage. Unlike other parts of the body, most cells in the brain cannot renew or repair themselves.[16]

After being privy to this information, I said to myself, you see this, I exhibited to a tee many of the RAD symptoms. No wonder I was such a mess—the wild, erratic behavioral swings, the incessant, inconsolable crying, the deficient social, vocal and motor skills, the bodily, mental and speech freezes, the day-dreaming and unaccountable passages of time, the aloofness, aloneness, and false self-sufficiency, the excruciating sense that something was wrong with me and that I wasn't who I was supposed to be and my futile attempts to fix me.

I said to myself, sometimes when we see children misbehaving, exhibiting antisocial behavior—alcohol and drug abuse, promiscuity, juvenile delinquency, violence, gang activity—we discard them as crazy, evil, *jemetes* (prostitutes), unredeemable, when it is none of the children's fault. They are just damaged people, trauma victims of physical, verbal or sexual abuse, parental separation or abandonment, etc. So what they need most is an abundance of love, empathy, understanding, therapy. Instead, what they get from us is rejection, vilification, and relegation to the scrap heap of human garbage. Life can be so very unfair.

It wasn't any more my fault that my mother left for England in the middle of our bonding than it was my fault that I was conceived and born. And a three-year-old can't be held responsible for his behavior, which is nothing but a reaction to the circumstances of his birth, nurturing and living conditions. And even though, thanks to the healing and coping powers of the human mind, the damaged three-year-old miraculously stays on the right side of the law as an adult and becomes a productive member of society, the internal quality of his life is forever compromised. After all, according to the research mentioned above, childhood trauma could cause irreversible brain damage.

I can well imagine my mother experiencing pangs of guilt about leaving her children behind in the care of others, even though the guardians were her father and sisters, her very own family, and even though it was to help prepare a better life for them. My mother's feelings of guilt were, I imagine, so pronounced that she couldn't stomach talking about this aspect of her emigration to England, so she consistently rebuffed anyone, including her own children, attempting to discuss or engage her on the matter.

My Mother's reticence about leaving her children behind and what happened to them in her absence left me frustrated and despondent. But with the onset of maturity and, more lately, during my mother's illness and continuing after her death, I gained a better understanding of why, besides guilt, she refused to revisit the past and subject herself to self-incrimination and the criticism of others. For how can you explain the matrix of emotions, personal ambition, personality traits, economic and social pressures, and the mores of the time that come to bear on the making of a decision or upon your conduct if the inquisitorial person wasn't there at the time thinking and feeling and exposed to all what you were experiencing? How can you adequately explain your actions to them? Doesn't that put you at a decisive disadvantage? More so since no matter how regrettable and unfortunate, the past cannot be undone.

Of course, this was understandable from my mother's vantage point; this was all fair and well for her, but to the inquiring person, her children especially, this disposition denied them understanding, closure, the materials for self-therapy, for coming to terms with who they are, where they come from, and the events and forces that have shaped their lives.

The Francis family is a traveling clan. Most of Mama Jonah and Papa Jonah's thirteen children have lived abroad (UK, USA, Guyana, Brazil). Seven of my mother's nine children have lived at least several years overseas (USA, USVI, Trinidad). The same pattern holds for most of the children of my aunts and uncles and deepens with each subsequent generation.

Understandably, my mother wasn't the only one to leave children behind. With all this traveling and emigration, some children of the Francis family were invariably left behind, often with tragic consequences. Several of the children left behind, even though they later joined their parents overseas or their parents returned home to be with them, succumbed to drug and alcohol abuse, delinquency, bouts with the criminal justice system, estrangement from their parents, and in a few cases, premature death.

When my mother returned from England, little three-year-old me rejected her, refused to accept her as my mother. But that was to be expected. The bond between mother and child wasn't firmly attached before the separation. But what surprised me was that sometimes it isn't the child who rejects the mother but the mother who denies the child. Some parents left their children behind, married in London, started a new family, and never looked back, for all practical purposes disowning, forever abandoning their first set of children. And there are some who, upon visiting home, took one look at their shabby, seemingly retarded, hookworm-infected children and found it difficult to bring themselves to accept that these children came from them. Some may continue to support their children financially but are glad to leave them permanently in the care of grandparents and return unencumbered to England to resume their lives. So apparently, the child-parent bond cuts both ways. Just as the child may never fully accept the mother as his mother when the mother-child bond didn't reach consummation, deep down the mother may never fully accept the child as hers.

The case of one of my cousins is instructive. Her mother, my aunt, left her and several of her siblings in the care of Mama Jonah in the vale in Desruisseaux and went overseas to work to better provide for her children. My cousin, the last child, was slightly over a year old when her mother left. She was in terrible shape. She would sit on a chamber pot all day long. Concerned that at this rate she would not survive, my mother took her niece under her wings. Apparently, because of her age she was still within the window of mother-child bonding; my cousin bonded securely with my mother. So much so that my cousin revealed that all the time she was living with us, she never thought or realized that her aunt wasn't her birth mother. I found this amazing because my cousin looks quite different from me and my siblings. My aunt married a man of Amerindian and European ancestry in Guyana, so her children's features reflect this mixed heritage.

My aunt returned when my cousin was in her early teens, and I'm sure she was looking forward to happily reuniting with her children. But by then she was a stranger to her daughter. Besides, as far as the daughter was concerned, she already had a mother whom she loved and to whom she was strongly and firmly attached. My cousin flat-out refused to join her biological mother until, finally, my mother compelled her to. Even so, she would invent all kinds of ex-

Magna a memoir of the enduring human spirit

cuses to stay with us after school (which was in Vieux Fort) instead of going home to her mother in Desruisseaux. My cousin said her mother's return damaged her life. She was forced to give up the mother she knew and loved for the stranger with whom she felt little connection and whom she distrusted. Unsurprisingly, her school grades plummeted, and she became rebellious and engaged in risky behavior. Her relationship with her mother remained problematic and mutually distrustful to the very end. Emotionally, she never stopped viewing her aunt as her birth mother.

Despite the obvious human cost of leaving children behind, the habit isn't frowned upon; it is still acceptable and sanctioned. On several occasions, I was privy to my mother advising, perhaps even encouraging mothers to leave their children behind and seek their fortunes overseas and thus put themselves in a better position to support their family, as if there was no downside to such a course of action. Yet there is little doubt that she was fully aware of the harmful effects of her London stint on her children. I contend that even though a parent concludes that this is the best course of action, they should be mindful of the potential harm and thus proceed in a manner that minimizes the damage.

It isn't only parents who are silent about or neglect to acknowledge the negative consequences of Caribbean migration on the children left behind. Social historian Dr. Jolien Harmsen, principal author of *A History of St. Lucia* (2012), the first and so far only attempt at a comprehensive history of St. Lucia, noted that academicians and public intellectuals have also neglected to focus on the children, the real victims (and ostensibly the intended beneficiaries) of these migrations.[17]

Much has been written about the social, economic and political aspects of West Indian labour migration over the years, but the crushing emotional impact it—occasionally—must have had, remains virtually invisible in both academic works and Caribbean literature. From my own work on intergenerational relations in Vieux Fort since 1910, I can testify to the profound long-term impact of the quality of emotional relationships between children and their caregivers on those children's future social, economic (financial) and educational development.

I IMAGINE THAT MY EXPERIENCE of separating from my mother when she left for England—the bewilderment, sense of abandonment, sense that my entire world had suddenly fallen apart—wasn't unlike that of my African forbears when out of the blue, without any warning whatsoever, they were suddenly seized from their village or their family compound, yoked with other captives from different villages, different tribes, marched to the coast to become cargo in the dark dungeon of slave ships, to then arrive in a strange land where toil and sweat were all they could look forward to, leaving them to wonder why their gods and ancestors had forsaken them. What crime, what atrocities had they committed to warrant this outrageous punishment? And what could they do to appease the gods and ancestors and make this predicament go away so they could return to the sanctuary of their family, their village, their homeland?

I also imagine that my foray into my past—relating my story and attempting to solve the riddles of my life, trying

Magna a memoir of the enduring human spirit

to fix me, attempting to make me whole—including the writing of this memoir and the one before it, *My Father Is No Longer There*, is not unlike the earlier activities of African diaspora people. They often conjured myths of portal-ling or teleporting back to Africa, and hatched such superstitious or supernatural beliefs as in *ladjablès, maman de l'eau, gen gagés,* and *ti boloms* to gain a sense of control over their lives. Likewise, to give meaning to their lives, to protect and preserve their identity, humanity, personhood, and sanity, they patched together fragments of their African languages and cultures, thus gaining a semblance of wholeness, and, in the process, gave rise to art and a novel worldview.

All this Walcott expressed beautifully in his Nobel Lecture, *The Antilles: Fragments of Epic Memory.*

Break a vase, and the love that reassembles the fragments is stronger than that love which took its symmetry for granted when it was whole. The glue that fits the pieces is the sealing of its original shape. It is such a love that reassembles our African and Asiatic fragments, the cracked heirlooms whose restoration shows its white scars. This gathering of broken pieces is the care and pain of the Antilles, and if the pieces are disparate, ill-fitting, they contain more pain than their original sculpture, those icons and sacred vessels taken for granted in their ancestral places. Antillean art is this restoration of our shattered histories, our shards of vocabulary, our archipelago becoming a synonym for pieces broken off from the original continent.

London Calling

There is evidence to suggest that traumatic experiences are often transferred from one generation to the next and can become the shared reality of a whole group of people.[18] Now, I wasn't surprised that such intergenerational or transgenerational trauma can be reinforced and transmitted through environmental, psychological, and social means. But what surprised me was that the transference can occur biologically. For example, maternal stress-related chemicals can impact the development of the fetus, and traumatic experiences can cause epigenetic changes that affect how the genes work, which are then passed on to future generations.[19,20]

Research has established that intergenerational trauma arising from slavery and post-slavery structural racism has made African Americans more vulnerable to such undesirable health outcomes as anxiety, depression, high blood pressure, obesity, diabetes, and cardiovascular diseases.[16] And some researchers have posited that the chronic stress and nutritional deficiencies that African Americans suffered during slavery may have induced epigenetic changes that have compromised their physical and mental health.[21]

Of course, on the flip side, one can entertain the notion that the practice of racism is also a form of trauma and mental disorder that has induced intergenerational and possibly transgenerational maladaptive behaviors and dysfunctional attitudes and habits among Whites. Toni Morrison, for example, said:

> The people ... who practice racism are bereft, there is something distorted about the psyche, it's a huge waste and it's a corruption and a distortion, it's like it's a pro-

Magna a memoir of the enduring human spirit

found neurosis...it has just as much of a deleterious effect on white people, and possibly equal as it does black people. [22]

Notwithstanding, all this made me wonder whether the St. Lucian and West Indian predilection to emigrating, which most times means separation from spouse and children and attendant detrimental consequences, is simply a matter of survival, a matter of circumventing their homeland's limited opportunities, dire socioeconomic conditions, and tiny landmass that forces them to be outward-looking.

Or is it also yet another legacy of slavery and post-slavery blues, yet another manifestation of cultural trauma? African Atlantic enslavement meant a forceful separation from all that the captives held dear; it was collective damage, trauma, and physical and psychological abuse to the extreme. So could it be that the enslavement trauma of forced separation from homeland and family (combined with the fact that slavery, a condition in which one's spouse and children were the property of others to do with as they will, was inimical to family life and familial bonds) made emigration, the leaving behind of spouse and children, a more acceptable or comfortable behavioral pattern among the descendants of the enslaved, to become a cultural meme, yet another manifestation of intergenerational trauma?

Magna in her 80s before she fell ill
and became bedridden

CHAPTER THIRTEEN

As My Mother Lay Dying

MY BEDROOM, which doubles as my office and where I do most of my writing, is next to my mother's. So I'm close at hand to assist my sister. She needs my help to put my mother in the wheelchair and to take her to the veranda. She also needs my help to shift and hold her in desired positions when changing her diaper, treating her bedsores, or giving her a bed bath. We keep her bedroom door open, so I hear when she is praying or talking to herself or screaming or calling for help.

Even with my help, caring for my mother must be both physically and emotionally draining for my sister. More so that my mother resists being moved and shifted, insists on having her way, of being in charge, and behaves in a very entitled manner with no qualms about laying the guilt trip thick and heavy—"Lord, have pity on me. *Yo ka fè mwem méchansté,* they are abusing me."

The nurses at St. Jude Hospital would likely attest to my mother's entitled and bossy behavior. About three years after my mother's death, her eldest sibling was hospitalized, and her foot was amputated because poor blood circulation had caused gangrene to set in. Upon visiting their mother at the hospital, my cousins apologized to the nurses for their mother giving them a hard time. One of the nurses responded with something akin to, "Oh, no; on the contrary, your mother hasn't given us any trouble. It was the other lady, Mrs. Reynolds; she was the difficult one; she was the troublemaker. Compared to her, your mother is an angel. That Mrs. Reynolds, I've never had a patient as rude and bossy as she."

Despite being at the hospital in a medical ward full of patients, everyone within earshot burst out laughing.

Of course, as my brother Prosper surmised, some of what was perceived as bossy or rude may just have been my mother's unwillingness to accept inferior care.

In the months immediately following my mother's return home from the hospital, she used to call out to us throughout the day and occasionally during the night. I was well up to the challenge of assisting my sister. But the constant calling and complaining and screaming were alarming and emotionally taxing, undermining both my ability to work and the quality of my sleep. For weeks, I gave up on work and slept fitfully.

Now, after about a year at home, it's not as bad. She is no longer screaming. She calls mostly for water. To give her water, we hold the water bottle for her, and she drinks from a straw. I suspect that when she calls, it isn't necessarily out of a need for water, even though that's what she requested. She drifts in and out of sleep, so sometimes, on waking, she is disoriented, unsure where she is and what's happening to her, so she desires the company of her children for reassurance.

From my bedroom and sometimes at her bedside, I hear her praying, chanting, or repeating a mantra. "Lord, forgive me for all my sins. Lord, have mercy on my poor soul."

I'm a backslider from the Adventist faith and, for that matter, from Christianity. I don't follow any religion and question the existence of God. But listening to my mother praying to her God, I can see the value of religion, of believing in God. In this, the lowest point in her life, when she is as helpless as a newborn, it must be a tremendous source of comfort, of healing, to know that an all-powerful being, the ultimate healer, is looking after her. That she can leave it all in His hands; that no matter how low, how bad, how painful, He will take care of her. And she need not worry because when all fails, she has an unbelievable place waiting for her on the other side of the river where, among many privileges, she will get to fellowship with Him face to face.

There was plenty of singing at the funeral and burial service of my father. I must admit that the singing was so soothing, so comforting, so in tune, so in step with my feelings at the time that even though I am a non-believer, I was full of gratitude for the Adventist folk. No matter my personal beliefs and attitude toward God and religion, I would never want to take anyone's religion away from them. I was glad that in my mom's greatest need, she could call on someone and, in the very process of calling upon him, gain peace, assurance and comfort. I also thought it was wonderful and of great value to be part of a religious or social group such as the Seventh-Day Adventist, for the congregation was an instant support group, an instant spring of sustenance and strength.

As my mother could no longer attend church, a group from the congregation came to fellowship with her every Saturday. They conducted church service right there in her bedroom while she lay helpless, but I bet thankful for the fellowship and heavenly blessings. They sang, read Scriptures, and prayed to their God to heal their sister in Christ and give her the strength and courage she needed to persevere. And I can tell in their passionate singing and emotional prayers that they truly believed God would intervene. I never joined these church services, but could hear them from my bedroom/office. I must say the service soothed and comforted me. After all, it was my mother in there. No matter that my sleep and work were suffering, I was willing to give up much more to keep her around as long as possible, so I was very welcoming of all the help on offer, even from the God and religion I was skeptical of and estranged from.

Sometimes, when listening to and being comforted by the service, I couldn't help but contemplate the power of religion. There is a dimension to human beings that seems beyond the physical. A dimension that, in moments of our greatest need, enables us to go beyond the possible, beyond human strength and endurance, and perform remarkable and impossible feats of survival. Maybe that dimension is what is called the human spirit. Religions of all kinds and all strains seem to have been created and evolved to tap into this hidden and unsuspecting wellspring of fortitude.

Is this at least partly where the concept of God came from? Why is there an innate spiritual or religious need in humans? Or, in other words, of what survival value is that trait? The theory of evolution would suggest that the prevalence of this human trait implies that individuals who carried the gene or genes that made them prone to spirituality and religiosity were more likely to survive into adulthood than their non-spiritual counterparts, so over time the human population came to be comprised mostly of people carrying the spiritual gene.

I prefer to think of the human spirit as a manifestation of the subconscious mind, the hidden spring that when tapped into can turn us into seemingly superhuman, supernatural forces. And that is what I suspect religion has tapped into, as have other areas of human endeavor. But how does it do that? Well, I believe that all forms of prayers, chants, mantras, meditation routines, ritual dances, certain kinds of music, etc., are tools used by religion, medicine, the military, etc., to access the powers of the subconscious, to heal the sick, to gain courage for the battlefield, to keep going even when it seems pointless to do so. Certain drugs also facilitate access to the subconscious, so it is no surprise that some shamans employ drugs in their religious rituals and divinations. I suspect that much of sports psychology has to do with the tapping of the subconscious mind. I also suspect there may be some validity to group subconscious, where under certain conditions our subconscious minds are shared and linked. So the collective performance of the group, the team, the battalion, is greater than the sum of their individual performances. This is consistent with the findings of cognitive scientists Steven Sloman and Philip Fernbach,[23] that the communal nature of human intelligence and knowledge has given individuals the illusion that they know more than they do.

As My Mother Lay Dying

I doubt that, as the Adventist Brethren were fellowshipping with my mother in her days of greatest need, they were thinking of any of this. But I was grateful for their intervention and what it meant to my mother. They helped her access her internal resources, the reservoir she needed to continue holding on to life.

Nonetheless, the heathen in me made me wonder whether in my mother's lucid moments she didn't begrudge God even a little. After all, her husband was killed two decades ago in the most inglorious manner, reduced to a useless paper doll by a reckless motorist. And here she was, mired in the indignity of bedsores, bed-boundedness and helplessness. This doesn't seem just reward for their steadfastness in Christ and for having shepherded the flock and stewarded the vineyard. But on second thought, I doubt she would have even an iota of misgivings about her God. Much like casinos, Christianity, or rather religion as a whole, is rigged for God to always come out on top. If one recovers from sickness, *praise the Lord; God is good.* If instead one succumbs to illness, *be comforted, for God knows best.* Regardless of the outcome, God hails supreme. In the case of my parents, I wished God had lost this once, for both still had plenty to live for, and if not for the mishaps—auto accident and pneumonia—they would have lived a few more good years.

My mother was also thrilled when my oldest brother (her oldest child) and his wife visited (they live in Balata, Babonneau, at the opposite end of the island). I, too, welcome their visits. He brings a different kind of energy into the picture, a proactive, uplifting energy, and his wife adores my mother. They are well connected, my mother and her oldest child. They see eye to eye; they share similar values, beliefs, sensibilities. He was nine years old when she left for England, so he had ample time to bond with her before her departure. He is much more empathetic toward her than I am. Unlike me, he would never tell her things like, *Ma Sido, you behaving like a big baby.* Whatever she says or demands, he takes it at face value and does his best to comply, to appease. A comparison of how the two of us relate to our mother highlights the difference between complete and incomplete bonding. Emotionally, he is much more in tune with her.

My youngest sister, a retired secondary school teacher and now a part-time behavioral counselor, lives a few minutes' drive away with her husband and three adult children. She is about a year and a half my senior. She comes and stays on some weekends to give my eldest sister a well-deserved break. She completely takes over, doing everything her sister does for my mother, including cooking and administering all the requisite care.

She was no older than two years and six months when our mother left for England, so like me, she wouldn't have had time to fully bond with her before she departed. And like me, I suspect her incomplete bonding is reflected in how she relates to and takes care of our mother. Her approach is much more matter-of-fact than her sister's, more like the way hospital nurses care for their patients. She is much less indulgent of her and much less tolerant of her non-cooperation, her attempts at having her way, and her nagging, which seems designed to instill guilt. And, of course, being in the same boat as my youngest sister regarding our emotional connection with our mother, I agreed with her approach and disposition. After all, I thought my eldest sister was too lenient with my mother, too accommodating to her every whim. So much so that I would remind her that our mother is now like a baby, and like a baby we can't trust that she always knows what's best, so we can't give in to everything she wants or demands. We are now the parents, and she the child, the baby.

Once, to make my point, I said, "Zel, take, for example, a baby crying for a knife. Would you give the baby the knife simply because she is crying and screaming for it?"

My kind, meek, benevolent sister would smile, provide no words of protest or disagreement, but would continue with no change of disposition toward her mother. Saying, in effect, *what do logic and reasoning have to do with feelings, with emotions, with love?* She was eight years old when my mother departed for England, so, like my eldest brother, she was fully bonded with my mother. They were like sisters, best friends.

Unlike my mother, my youngest sister had never separated from her three children while they were young. And it shows. The children appear well-bonded with their mother. They are like best friends. They seem very close and emotionally connected to her. My sister seems to enjoy a much closer relationship with her kids than my mother with hers. I suspect that with her kids my sister has overcompensated for what may have been lacking in her relationship with her mother.

Nonetheless, when my mother complained and fussed about the care she was receiving, I would jokingly tell her, "Ma Sido, you there complaining and complaining, but you don't know how lucky you are. You have your very own private nurse and your nine children doting over you. I will never be as lucky as you."

Most times she simply ignored me and continued fussing. But all joking aside, it seemed to me that the personalized, patient-centered care and the unconditional love and support of family, friends, neighbors, and community that my mother was receiving, as well as her tapping into her faith as a source of solace and fortitude, seemed exactly what holistic care would have ordered and probably account for how long she was able to hold on.

In my mother's active life, she was a giver and a keeper; in her moment of greatest need, her bigheartedness was rewarded abundantly. *Give, and it shall be given unto you.* Truer words were never spoken, at least with regard to my mother.

CHAPTER FOURTEEN

The Story of My Life

EVERYONE HAS A STORY TO TELL, an often-repeated narrative, usually rooted in childhood, that defines who they are, shapes their lives, colors their very existence. A story that's reflected in every word they speak, every decision they make, every action they take. A story that stands out above all others. And no matter the person, they don't have to know you too well or for too long before they let the story out, for the story is always waiting for an opportunity to be heard. It can't be silenced any more than roosters announcing the break of day, *bètafé* from lighting the night, crickets from disturbing the peace of the evening. Yet the story has no satisfactory resolution, and its telling only brings fleeting relief, fleeting fulfillment.

I suspect my father's story was that someone or another was always taking advantage of him, but he chose to look the other way. He had a John Wayne, Clint Eastwood, Jason Statham kind of bravery and heroism, especially when it came to protecting his loved ones, but he turned the other cheek, not out of cowardice or weakness, but for the sake of maintaining the peace and safeguarding his peace of mind.

On the other hand, I suspect my mother's story was that she was unloved, unappreciated. She would complain that someone or the other didn't want her, didn't love her, which was amazing because she always had lots of people—relatives, friends, neighbors, brothers and sisters of her Adventist faith, the young, the old, the not so young—visiting her, spending plenty of time with her. Yet she would single out the few who didn't take to her as much as she would have liked or whom it seemed didn't visit or call her as often as she thought they should. "*Fanm sala pa enmen mwen pyès*; this woman doesn't like me at all." "*Fanm sala pa vlé mwen*; this woman doesn't care about me."

During my mother's illness, anytime she didn't get her way, or we were too slow responding to her requests, she would put the guilt trip on us by accusing us of not loving her. "Anderson, *mwen za sav ou pa enmen mwen*; Anderson, I already know you don't love me." Or, "Ezildra, *mwen pa sav sa mwen fè'w, mé ou pa enmem mwen ankò*; Ezildra, I don't know what I did you, but you don't love me anymore."

At such times, I would be thinking, "You are on the last leg of your life, so why should it matter that we love or don't love you? What's important? Isn't it that we are taking good care of you?"

I wondered what it is about love that makes people, even on their deathbeds, a few breaths away from their demise, still seek it, still concerned with whether someone loves them or not. Why is love so important, or rather, why is the knowledge that we are loved so critical that we will do anything for it? Without it we are likely to self-destruct; life seems not worth living; life seems meaningless. Is it because

The Story of My Life

it has survival value, the spark that compels us to go beyond the impossible to keep the people we love alive, so instinctively we know that our survival, the very existence of our species, is predicated on love? Thus deep down, we know that without it, we are doomed.

Or is it simply that during an earlier evolutionary phase, individuals who carried the love gene (and so were the ones who sought love and loved others) were those who were more likely to survive into adulthood and thus were the ones who were able to pass on their genetic material (including the love gene) to the next generation, so over time the human population became predominantly comprised of people carrying the love gene?

Unquestioningly, my story was centered around my relationship or rather my non-relationship with my mother—the separation, my perceived no-love-lost between us. One characteristic of the *story of your life* is that it never wears out, at least not on its wearer. So you shouldn't be surprised that even though I have already told the story of my life in my previous memoir, *My Father Is No Longer There*, I am here at it again.

As my mother lay in bed with her strong sense of entitlement, bossing my sister around, refusing to do for herself some of the things she was capable of doing, in continuation of our back-and-forth banter, I would tell her, "Ma Sido, you eh a baby, you know, so stop behaving like one." She would counter with, "Anderson, *mwen sé manman'w, ou sav;* Anderson, I'm your mother, you know." And to me that said it all, captured, summarized, the full essence of our historical relationship. It spoke to the tenuous bond between us, or what I once thought was tenuous.

Magna a memoir of the enduring human spirit

My mother's love, my mother's relationships, were a mixture of push and pull. She takes charge, caters to your needs, safeguards your well-being, but demands obedience, total submission, eating-out-of-her-hands. If she perceives challenge or animosity, her guards are up; her weapons are sharpened and on alert. I suspect that my predisposition toward her of distrust, disobedience, and viewing her as an enemy to pit my will against led to our muddled relationship. If other siblings enjoyed a more harmonious relationship with her, it may not have been because she favored them over me but because they presented themselves in a manner that elicited more favorable reactions.

I suppose that not being adequately bonded with one's mother, as I was, causes one's mind to throw up obstacles to prevent closeness. It's as if one's mind fears the potential negative consequences of the intimacy, fears another abandonment. It remembers too well the excruciating hurt and misery of the original separation. So, in self-defense, it throws up walls between one and one's mother.

As a child, I saw my mother as an enemy to pit my will against, to defy as much as I could. I didn't accept her as my mother; she couldn't be my mother. I didn't want her as my mother. She was an imposter.

Thus, growing up, I stayed away from her as much as possible. I never voluntarily sat on her lap or came anywhere close to her. I wondered how the other children could stomach being near her: sitting on her lap, resting on her, playing with her. In her presence, I was in dread; I was a prisoner, a mental cripple with no freedom. As a toddler my younger brother would wail when our mother was leaving the house without him. I never understood why he

The Story of My Life

wasn't jumping for joy that our mother was going away, and hence freedom. Freedom indeed, because I was told that when my mother was away, I became a menace. I got bold and wild and talkative and boastful and displayed such anti-social behavior as pelting stones after people. But when she was home, I was so docile, so in-my-shell, that people would pity me. "*Pòdjab*, Anderson, *pòdjab*."

My mother would tell them something akin to, "Don't worry yourself with him; just wait when I leave the house and see who you will pity."

When my mother passed, I thought I would be filled with regret for the way I had behaved towards her (even though over the years our relationship had kept improving), regret for some of the hurtful things I had said to her (of course, she meted out her fair share of hurt), regret for the times I had ignored her calls because I thought she was being too demanding. I expected to regret that I hadn't treated her with greater empathy, hadn't loved her as much as I should, hadn't taken better care of her as she lay dying. Strangely, I felt almost no guilt or remorse; I felt good about myself and my mother. I harbored warm and tender feelings toward her. I was proud of my mother and proud of being her son.

My aunt, who complained that my parents, my mother especially, mistreated her when she lived with us, said to me something like, "You see how life is? You and your mother didn't get along too well. But look, you are the one there with her, helping to care for her. If she had been more loving to you, I bet you would have been even more willing to look after her."

Magna a memoir of the enduring human spirit

The irony of it wasn't lost on me either. I was probably the last sibling someone would have picked as the one who would be with my mother in her days of greatest need. However, looking back, ironical or not, I have no regrets. I'm glad I could be with my mother, even though sometimes grudgingly, as a way of paying back the great sacrifices she had made for me and my siblings. In many ways it was a blessing to be home with her during the last fifteen years of her life. This enabled me to gain a better understanding and appreciation of who she was, and, by the opportunity to observe up close the example of her life, I was privy to invaluable lessons on dying, on how best to live a life, on how to live a productive life in old age.

I was glad to be there, not just for my mother but also for my sister, my mother's main caregiver. If I had left, changed residence, I would have abandoned not just my mother but also my sister who has made her fair share of sacrifices for the family.

It seems my behavior toward my mother stemmed from my preconceived notion that she didn't love me. Perhaps, yet another wall I had put up. I hadn't realized how much I loved her and how much I wanted and needed her to love me.

When I went to the florist to order floral arrangements for my mother's funeral and burial, the florist asked me if I was the last child, the one my mother spoiled. I was taken aback because given the rocky, somewhat distant relationship I once had with my mother, I couldn't have been the spoiled one. Besides, the only time I was the last child was before my mother left for England. When she returned, I was no longer the last child because she was accompanied

The Story of My Life

by my ten-month-old brother. So I had to conclude that it was the emotion in my voice, the care and attention I gave to the selection of the wreaths, and my concern that the flowers be delivered on time that led the florist to that conclusion.

Still, I should have taken it as a hint that my love for my mother was more apparent than I thought. After all, in my late thirties, I penned a poem suggesting that my relationship with my mother was well on the mend. And as I started writing about her, the feelings that washed over me, mostly warm and pleasant, with few misgivings and incriminations, made me realize that all along I had loved my mother a great deal, and I probably haven't loved anyone else as much. So in much the same way that it was after my father's accidental death that the realization I didn't know him as well as a son should came in full force, it was only after my mother's death and in the process of writing about her that I fully realized the extent to which I loved her and was in awe of her.

At the time of my father's untimely death, I felt very protective of my mother; I stayed by her side as much as possible. It was as if I sensed that her life was in clear and imminent danger. As if the head of the mafia organization, my father, had been gunned down, and my mother, the new head, was in danger of the same treatment, but the organization couldn't survive another such devastating loss. So I needed to protect my mother at all costs, even with my own life. This was the predominant feeling or disposition that washed over me throughout the funeral and burial ceremonies and months after. That feeling I had towards my mother should have served as another hint, another indication of how much I loved her and how much I feared losing her.

I suspect the intensity of the hurt I suffered when my mother departed for London was so severe that thereafter, like a nut, I had developed a protective shell that was difficult to penetrate, that allowed my emotional core to surface only under such extreme conditions as the threat of my mother's death when the ambulance was taking her to hospital. It seems only under such extreme conditions, measured in moments, that the protective shell would crack to expose and access the kernel of love, bonding and trust between my mother and me during my first year of life before she left for London. Apparently, that kernel has always been there and will always be there, and maybe that's why therapy is so essential; perhaps it helps the patient to pry open the outer shell to get to that kernel and to build and enlarge upon it, to make it blossom and full one's being.

I must have loved my mother so dearly that I couldn't risk abandonment a second time, so I sprang up a jungle between us to prevent closeness. In hindsight, it would appear that a lot of my childhood and young adult self-defeating and self-destructive behavior was a reaction to my belief that my mother didn't love me, that no one loves me.

It seems I had steeled myself not to love my mother. But it appears that I was the only one deceived. I hadn't deceived the people around me, nor had I deceived my mother. Without me knowing, in my voice and involuntary actions, I was saying loud and clear that I love my mother, and my mother was probably saying in various ways that she loves me. I just had to open the door and let her love flow in. In any event, this is my preferred narrative.

The Story of My Life

The truth is, whether I like it or not, in myriad ways, the story of my life was intertwined with that of my mother. I suspect both our stories were about the fear of rejection, abandonment, and a craving for love and belonging.

If genuine love can only be measured not by words or emotional displays or lavish untestable promises but by the sacrifices we make and are willing to make for the ones we love, then my mother's love for her children, including me, was bottomless. My brother said it best in his eulogy to my father, which I think applies equally to my mother.

Our father embraced his responsibilities to his family without reservation. His love and devotion to us were not typically expressed via grand gestures or flamboyant demonstrations of affection. Instead, the depth of his love and commitment to us was left to be inferred from his daily devotion and determination to make any sacrifice and bear numerous burdens in the performance of his duty as both husband and father...In a world in which we are increasingly inundated with images of grandeur and flamboyance, and in which occasional and flamboyant demonstrations of affection threaten to substitute for the things that make families work—such as acceptance of responsibility and devotion to duty—our father opted in favor of daily devotion to duty.

Unlike me, my brother had gotten it right all along. People spend fortunes traveling around the world in search of love, in search of the meaning of love, often looking in all the wrong places, but here were my parents, living manifestations of what people were so desperately seeking. And

Magna a memoir of the enduring human spirit

maybe this was the ultimate and most important lesson my mother's life taught me—the meaning of love.

Finally, further expounding on the story of my life, I offer a poem I wrote in my late thirties, *The Child and His Mother*, tracing the history of my relationship with my mother or, at the very least, the direction I wanted the narrative to take. My willingness to share it reemphasizes the point that one never gets tired of sharing the story of one's life.

The mother, so dominating, so powerful, so
    intimidating
The mother, eyes sharp as an eagle's
Nothing is missed, everything is suspect,
Everything comes under scrutiny, eyes blazing
The child, so afraid of the mother,
So uncomfortable in her presence
What an ordeal to be in her presence
What a load a child who still wets his bed must carry
Stress of unimaginable proportions
The child is a stranger in his own home
No, the child is a prisoner in his own home
The child's bonding with the mother is incomplete
The child was born sickly
The child needed the mother more than most
The mother was the child's world
The child was inseparable from the mother
The child and the mother were one

Then like Africa, her children taken into bondage,
The mother departed from the child

The parting severed the child's heart in two,
Like two halves of a calabash
Never to completely make whole again
Never to complete the mother-child bond
Mother returns
The child is now three years old
But to the child many lifetimes have passed
Irreparable damage has been done
The child is never to trust anyone with the profundity
With which he once trusted his mother
The child has learned too well
The mother appears as if by magic
On a horse-drawn carriage
Dressed in finery white:
White gloves, white high-heel shoes
White wide-brim hat covered with a velvet veil
To the child she is from another world
She, so full of life and zest,
Looks down with piercing eyes
Disapprovingly on the skinny, malnourished child
She left behind in the care of others
The custodians of her child have done him injustice
Her eyes watery,
She is filled with anger, pity, and guilt
It has been one assault after another
Mother severing his heart in two
His custodians mistreating him like an unwanted
     orphan
His mistrust is complete
He accepts not his mother
Instead he goes around asking others

Magna a memoir of the enduring human spirit

If they were his mother
He is more accepting of strangers than of his own
To add insult to injury
Mother arrives with a substitute—
The child's youngest sibling
Sibling hanging onto mother's skirt
As if to let go is to sign a death warrant
There is no more room for the child
Competition has arrived

Love is a two-way street
The child has rejected his mother
Mother is appalled, hurt, and filled with remorse
The child is bleeding inside
Mother responds to the rejection
With annoyance, frustration, and vexation
What a tragedy
What the child needs most is love and affection
More than ever
Large doses of love and affection
The child needs to overcome
His distrust and to love again
But he receives the opposite
Mother has become his enemy
The child is only three years old
He does not know how to love or how to be loved
He knows not how to express affection
The child is twisted
He is tied into knots upon knots of emotions
The mother spends many sleepless nights
Wanting so much to rekindle and complete

The Story of My Life

The bond she had left incomplete
But the child refuses the offer
He has misjudged his mother
He has learned too well
He refuses to open up
His body and mind are trapped frozen
In a wintry, desolate land
His mother's efforts fall on barren soil
He does not want his heart splintered in two a second
      time
He knows not how to love
But love he is full of
So much is bottled inside
Like a river, his love flows but never reaches the ocean
Along the way the river has too many twists
And turns and dams to navigate
The child, not unlike the desire of descendants of the
Africans taken into bondage to reconnect with their
Ancestors, wants nothing more than to
Complete the mother-child bond
He wants nothing more but to run
Into his mother's arms and be comforted
Be reassured that everything will be alright
The mother like the father of the prodigal son
Wants nothing more than to open her arms
And let her son come home and fill the hole
That remains in her bosom

At the age of nineteen
After many battles with his mother
After many rebellions

Magna a memoir of the enduring human spirit

After denouncing his mother's religion
After destroying his fear and discomfort of his mother
The child begins to embrace his mother
Where once he saw hate he started seeing love
Where once he saw cruelty and punishment
He started seeing caring
His mother's piercing, threatening eyes
Were becoming a shield of protection around him
At long last the bond that was shattered
Over seventeen years ago was on the mend
The weight of the world was slowly
Lifting off the child's shoulders

But in the middle of this healing the child,
Now a man, departed like his mother before him
For foreign soil in search of education, career and
    wealth
A full circle
Now, after traversing a continent
After ten years of college the child realizes
That his search for education, career, and wealth
Was, in disguise, a search for his relationship with
    himself,
His mother, his immediate and extended family,
His country, his race, the motherland, the world.
Peace has settled
With knowledge has come understanding
With understanding has come tolerance,
Compassion and forgiveness
With understanding, tolerance, compassion,
And forgiveness has come love

The Story of My Life

The child's relationship with his mother has
Now blossomed like a flowering cactus in the Sahara
Where once there was tension
There is warmth and calm
Where once there was distrust,
There is love and understanding
Where once there was silence and brooding,
There is laughter and joy
All's well that ends well
But what a journey

Portrait of Magna by her grandson,
concept artist Afferton Raynold

CHAPTER FIFTEEN

How to Live a Healthy and Productive Life in Old Age

WHEN I RETURNED TO ST. LUCIA from my twenty-year North American sojourn, I ended up living with my parents. As expected, the usual adult-child-parent frictions surfaced. I complained to a cousin visiting from the US about my mother, but he was very unsympathetic; he showed no empathy. He said, "What do you expect, mature, grown-ass man like you still living with your parents? You need to find your own place and give the people their space."

Of course, his forthright advice, which even had a rhyme, embarrassed me, showed me up, left me with nowhere to hide. He was right, though; the fault was mine, all mine. I had no business living with my parents, especially after three decades of living on my own. It was I interfering with their program, interrupting their daily routine, the rhythm of their life.

But all things considered, it was a privilege, a blessing in disguise, living with my mom for most of the last twenty years of her life, including her nearly four years of being confined to her bed. I was afforded the opportunity to observe her up close and to reflect on her life. As a mature adult with acquired analytical skills, I was struck by the realization that there was much to glean from her example of how best to live a life.

In the final episode of the Spanish TV drama series *The Vineyard,* responding to his father (the protagonist) being called a coward and a lousy father who failed to secure his children's inheritance, the adult son said, "On the contrary...our father left us something more valuable than his property—a lesson on life. And we are very proud of him."

This sentiment couldn't have been more applicable to my mother and how I feel about her life. And perhaps the most pertinent lesson that I learned from the example of my mother's life is how to live a healthy and productive life in old age.

When my parents were well into their sixties, they moved to St. Jude's Highway on the outskirts of Vieux Fort. There, besides turning every inch of the yard not devoted to footpaths into a garden and going aerial with boxes, old tires, and abandoned fridges, my mother extended her garden and fence to the strip of land between her property and St. Jude's Highway. And she would get very annoyed with passersby who thought the fruits were there for their picking because the strip wasn't part of her land. She would say something like, "People really indiscreet; they think the garden came up all by itself."

I have a diploma in general agriculture from a once-upon-a-time agricultural school at Union, Castries. And my doctorate is in agricultural economics, which my alma mater, the University of Florida, calls food and resource

How to Live a Healthy and Productive Life in Old Age

economics. My mother would jokingly tell me something like, "Anderson says he is an agriculturist, but he isn't planting not even one lime tree. I don't understand what kind of agriculturist he is."

Looking back, I should probably have told her that one agriculturist, meaning her, was more than enough for the family.

My elderly mother would leave her bedroom every morning at around 6:30 without fail. By then, she would have already studied her Bible lesson and said her morning prayers. She would prepare her breakfast and set it aside for when she was ready to eat. Then she would set upon her gardening project, weeding, planting, harvesting, spreading manure or seaweed, commissioning the building of seed beds and planting boxes. By 9 AM, she would have returned to the kitchen to start cooking lunch. While the food was on the fire, she'd return to her garden, with the result that sometimes the food got overcooked, burnt even, before she could get back to it.

In the movie *A Family Thing*, starring Robert Duvall and James Earl Jones, when asked about the bad luck he'd had in his life, the character Bill Watley, an only child with both parents killed by lightning on the same day at the same time when he was a teenager, said: "Being happy ain't nothing more than having something to look forward to, and helping your people to have something to look forward to. I reckon that's what gets me through till tomorrow."

Well, in my mother's golden years, she had her garden to look forward to every single day.

When my mother wasn't gardening, she was cleaning and rearranging furniture; or she was grinding and bottling

Magna a memoir of the enduring human spirit

nuts, cinnamon, turmeric, bay leaf, and other spices; or she was making tamarind balls and gooseberry and golden apple jams to sell or give to children, visiting friends, and relatives. Four years after the death of my mother and eight years since she had become bedridden, there is still a large jar of her well-preserved gooseberry jam in the fridge. In more ways than one, the legacy of my mother cannot be denied.

My mother always had an abundance of cashew nuts, walnuts, and peanuts because these were among the staple gifts her children living in America brought her on their visits home. She had difficulty eating these nuts, so she came up with the innovation of grinding them to mix with her oatmeal. I was happy to be stealing her ground nuts with which, following her example, I fortified my porridge. And now, continuing the tradition, besides the nuts, I'm adding cut fruits to my oatmeal and cold cereal.

In the past, my mother's industriousness was a matter of survival, of keeping her family afloat, but in her old age she was financially well taken care of by her children and nieces and nephews, so her assiduousness wasn't out of necessity but out of habit, having something to look forward to, following the biblical mandate of *Occupy till I come.* I have no doubt that my mother's gardening both enhanced and lengthened her life.

ONE OF THE THINGS that intrigued me most about my mother was her cognitive ability and her grip on life even as she entered her twilight years. She was a masterclass on being present, mindfulness, living in the moment, honoring the sentiment that everything that happens happens in the moment. Her senses always on alert, her sharp, piercing, unflinching, eagle eyes missing nothing. She placed things back exactly where she found them, switched off the light as she left the room, unplugged appliances from electric sockets right after use. She prepared for events way ahead of time. Meals were prepared hours before mealtime: breakfast by 7 AM, lunch by 10 AM, and dinner by 4 PM. And by 6:30 PM she would have had dinner and be relaxing in preparation for bed by 9 PM and to wake up at 5:30 AM.

I had a running joke with my mother about her sleep. Each morning she woke up, she would say, "I didn't sleep at all last night." I would retort with, "But Mama, if you were awake all night, what were you doing in bed all that time?"

Regarding preparation, my mother may have gotten that habit from Mama Jonah. I'm told that when my grandmother was going on a trip, she packed her grip three weeks beforehand.

My mother's attention to detail, to everything around her, applied to everyone in her purview. When I was leaving the house, she would call me out on issues with my attire: mismatched socks, shirt missing buttons, collar not tucked properly, clothes in need of ironing. She would also call attention to when I had worn the same clothes several times in a row or when it was the first time she saw me in an outfit. In exasperation, I would tell her, "Ma Sido, you paying me too much attention."

Of course, I now painfully miss this attention.

Perhaps part of the reason I was so intrigued by my mother's cognitive competence and why it stands out so much for me was that it brought to sharp relief my cognitive failures and inadequacies. I lacked my mother's mental cogency and agility, her sharp tongue, her command of the moment, her take-charge persona. As a child, I was dreamy and absent-minded. I kept losing my shoes, slate, pencils, exercise books, anything that wasn't directly attached to my body. I put my shoes on the wrong foot and my shirt on the wrong side. My shirt was always missing buttons. I was lousy at errands; I would likely forget some items on my shopping list and return with the wrong change. I was shy and tongue-tied. Sometimes, I froze in front of people, unable to answer questions. People thought I was either crazy or retarded or both. "*Tibway-la ka fou*, the boy is crazy," or "*Tibway-la tenbwé*, the boy is retarded," was how I was often characterized.

My eldest sister, Zel, complains that she is getting more forgetful with age. I would tell her, "I don't know about that because from the time I know myself, I have been forgetful. Even now, I can't wear things like watches and hats because I keep losing them. I cannot count the number of times I have lost and found my cell phone. But I'm getting better with age." I tell her that as a joke, but it's the truth.

Compared to my mother, I was a mess. But thanks to her example, I have made some improvements in my life.

MY MOTHER'S DAILY ROUTINE coincided with the cycles of nature, with the movements of the heavenly bodies. She rose with the morning sun, and as the sun proceeded to bury itself at the horizon, she ceased work and began the process of retiring for the night. Her sleep routine took full advantage of the 10 PM to 2 PM period during which the body is healing, mending itself.

In the same way my mother consulted the almanac to ensure that her planting schedule was aligned with nature, thus securing optimal yields, she made lifestyle choices conducive to good health and longevity. She didn't smoke or drink; she ate no meat, only fish. On Saturdays, following the dictates of her Seventh-Day Adventist faith, she withdrew from her worldly activities, and other than praising, acknowledging, and contemplating the handicraft of her God, she came to a complete rest of body and mind, thus getting a respite from the weekly grind and accumulated stress and refueling for the week ahead. She made a conscious effort to eat greens with her lunch and some fruit with her breakfast. Whether walking around the house, working in her garden, riding a stationary bicycle, or joining the Three Angels Broadcasting Network (3ABN) morning workout show, she made a conscious effort to exercise daily.

Noticing the zeal with which she followed the 3ABN fitness workout, I would tease her, telling her there were other exercise programs on television that may be even better than 3ABN's. Of course, as I expected, she paid me no mind. It was either the 3ABN program or none at all. Adventists are clannish that way. It is my impression that they are reluctant to read non-Adventist literature, participate in non-Adventist events or activities, and some even have difficulty making friends with non-Adventists.

My mother was a walking manual on how to live with and manage a serious health condition. She lived with diabetes for over fifty years, but didn't let that stop her from living a full life. She managed her health and medical condition with regular exercise, proper sleep, and a healthy, meatless diet. It also helped that she was very nearly a bush doctor, with the medicinal herbs and plants growing right there in her garden, and her eldest daughter, a registered nurse, was readily available to help monitor her vital signs and administer medication.

However, my mother wasn't infallible. Every so often, she would pledge to follow a strictly vegetarian diet—no fish, no dairy—only to be happily eating fish a week later. She went through this cycle so often that I started teasing her about it.

My mother had a friend with a critical case of kidney stones whose doctor was recommending laser treatment. My mother prescribed a tea drawn from *gwenn anba fèy*, a medicinal herb growing in her yard. After a few days of the herbal tea, the kidney stones melted away, leaving the friend's doctor in disbelief.

My mother loved doctor visits. I have never encountered anyone who relished doctors' visits as much as she did. I reckoned it was the dressing up and the attention that accompanied the visits that did it for her. After each appointment, she always had stories to tell. Yet she didn't rely solely on doctors or put all her faith in them. She approached all prescribed medication with caution and reservation. Once, her doctor prescribed a high blood pressure medication; I suspect she was a borderline case. She put aside the drugs and started taking garlic tablets for the condition, which seemed to work because on her subsequent visits to the doctor, her readings were normal. She stayed with the garlic tablets at the exclusion of the prescription, the doctor being none the wiser.

My health-conscious, elderly mother said that she had a dream in which someone told her that she must stop

How to Live a Healthy and Productive Life in Old Age

drinking water from plastic bottles because the chemicals from the plastic seep into the water. In the dream, the person pointed to several one-gallon glass bottles. The following morning, a neighbor came by with three of the type of bottles my mother had seen in her dream, hoping my mother could find use for them. From that day on, my mother stopped drinking from plastic bottles; for potable water, she boiled tap water and stored it in the glass bottles.

Observing all the care and attention my eighty-something mother paid to her health, I would smile and say to myself, "Eh-eh, Ma Sido thinks she is going to live forever!"

We don't live forever, but it is the responsibility and prerogative of every person to try to live and enjoy a productive life as long as possible. My mother, I must say, gave it her best shot.

Besides her health, in her old age, my mother never stopped paying attention to her appearance. She delighted in dressing up for church, doctor's appointments, and other such outings. She would wear a wig and often a blue, flowery dress (I think blue was her favorite color). She didn't wear makeup because Adventists frowned upon such Jezebel-like practices, but her face was powdered, which softened her features. She would wear a radiant, happy, watch-me-am-I-not-pretty smile and ensure she was noticed by being chatty or asking you to zip her dress. When she returned home from these outings, no matter that you were there with her and privy to what transpired, she would eagerly relate and embellish the happenings of the outing, in which she invariably played the starring role, the heroine, either straightening out people or mesmerizing them with her wit, charm, and proactivity. At such times, I saw my mother in a very different light. With her softer, vain side exposed, it would occur to me that she wasn't just this fierce, formidable being but a woman and a person with all the attendant frailties and vulnerabilities. Even as my mother was bedridden and holding on to dear life, she was still particular about her appearance. She insisted on her hair being made and having a fresh gown every morning. This was yet another lesson my mother's life taught: grooming and paying attention to how one presents oneself is an essential part of fostering well-being and engendering sound mental health.

Another thought I had observing my mother's attempt at defeating old age and death was that people don't just die. We die of something; there is always a cause of death; we die from a condition or conditions. Of course, this is so obvious that it probably isn't worth repeating, except it suggests that if, with the help of diet and lifestyle changes, we can manage our medical conditions, then, like my mother, we give ourselves the best chance of living long and productive lives.

My mother's religion helps explain her health consciousness. It is rare to run into an Adventist who isn't health-conscious. In fact, they have no choice but to be health conscious, for they take to heart the Apostle Paul's notion in First Corinthians 3:17 that their bodies are the temple of God and not theirs to treat as they please, and so they must take care not to defile their bodies. Growing up in the church, from weekly Bible lessons, Saturday afternoon Young People Meetings, Sunday and Wednesday Prayer Meetings, and sermons from the pulpit or at crusades, I was inundated with healthy living admonishments—the necessity and value of proper posture, regular exercise, early to bed, fasting and praying, balanced meals, not eating meals-between-meals, not over-eating, being temperate in all things, a diet away from meat and towards grains, fruits, nuts, and vegetables, abstaining from smoking, alcohol, coffee and all substances that alter the mind, irritate or excite the nerves, adhering to Deuteronomy Chapter 14 on what was clean and good to eat and what was unclean and forbidden.

Besides the church services and programs, our home was crowded with the books (several of which were about healthy living and diet and foods) of Ellen G White, the Adventist prophetess whose writings Adventists hold nearly as sacred as the Bible. During the summer months, when school was out, Adventist colporteurs, invariably college students raising funds to cover their tuition, made house-to-house calls, ensuring my parents didn't miss out on opportunities to stock up on encyclopedias, Ellen G. White books, and other books on Adventist doctrine. So whether at home or at church, there was no escape from hearing or reading about healthy living practices.

Is it any wonder that Adventists like my mother live longer than the general population? Loma Linda, a small city in Southern California with a population of 25,000, one-third of which are Adventists, is considered one of the world's handful of "blue zones" where people live exceptionally long lives. A study[24] involving over 34,000 California Adventists revealed that non-vegetarian Adventist men live 7.3 years longer than other Californians, while the women live 4.4 years longer. The results were even more startling when only vegetarian Adventists were considered. Compared to the non-Adventist population, vegetarian Adventist men lived nine years longer and the women 6.1 years longer.

DESPITE MY MOTHER'S SEDULITY, she never lost sight of the notion that it's people who matter. As much as situations permitted, she actively kept in touch with her children, siblings, cousins, nephews, and nieces. She enthusiastically cultivated and maintained friendships and relationships with her neighbors and Adventist brethren. I would spend years barely noticing or interacting with my neighbors. Not my mother. She sought out her neighbors, offering them the fruits of her garden, the jams and spices of her assembly line. One way or the other, she would not be ignored; they would be enticed to interact with her. No matter how busy she was or what she was working on, when people stopped by to visit, she always engaged them; she never wasted an opportunity to establish and deepen rapport. Now, that doesn't necessarily mean she stopped what she was doing. She would more likely put the visitor to work right alongside her or continue her work while talking. But never would she give anyone, no matter how old, how young, how rich or poor, the impression she was too busy for conversation, for engagement.

My mother would often complain about someone: "She doesn't like me; I don't know what I did to her, but she doesn't come and see me at all."

Now I would be thinking, if the person isn't coming and visit, that means less distraction from whatever you were doing and having more time to yourself. But this might be the introvert in me talking. I like (or rather end up) spending a great deal of time alone. But for my mom, an extrovert who never tires of company, that was a non-starter. My mother had no choice but to feel that way. This was the story of her life.

By now, it may have become apparent that, without any conscious effort, my mother's life epitomized many famous sayings. *One hand can't clap. A stitch in time saves nine. Don't leave for tomorrow what you can do today. Spare the rod, spoil the child.*

My mom was a firm believer in reciprocating, in the notion that there is no free lunch. She is sure to find a way to return any good deed, be it providing a meal, gifting the fruits of her labor, or donating her time. She also believed in giving unto Cesar what belongs to Cesar and unto God what belongs to Him. Whether or not my mother could sell the products of her yard and kitchen, she placed a monetary value on them and religiously paid the church her 10 to 20 percent tithe and offerings. She didn't earn much money, so most of these tithe and offerings came from funds received from her children and nieces and nephews. My mom grew up in an era when most people were barely getting by, when people had to make do without money, and when *koudmen, susu or béja, journées prêtées,* and barter were a big part of survival. So the proverb *one hand can't clap* would have been well ingrained in her.

My mother's life proves that *it is more blessed to give than to receive*; and *give, and it shall be given unto you.* But the lesson involved here goes beyond simply giving and receiving. As I'm entering old age, I'm realizing that people,

Magna a memoir of the enduring human spirit

including strangers, don't pay as much attention to me as in my younger days. There are now fewer stares. More and more, I'm ignored as if I'm not even there, as if I don't exist. I guess there is now less of what is to be admired. It is young people who are mostly up and about, and the young have eyes mostly for young people like themselves. Older adults are weird; they dress and talk funny and are not one's preferred option for sitting next to. *Don't get too close to them and risk their undesirableness, uncoolness, rubbing off on you.*

But remaining engaged with people, preferably of all ages and backgrounds, interacting, socializing, noticing others and being noticed by them, being wanted and needed, and remaining current are all critical for maintaining good mental health, especially in the case of older people. *What does a senior citizen have to do to get some attention?*

With such insights, I gained a better understanding and appreciation of how my mother lived her life. What better way to ensure your infant and teenage nieces and nephews flock to you and never forget you than always to have something nice and sweet for them and to constantly engage them? In the presence of my mother, there was no apathy. She engaged children, gave them things, got them to do things for her, joked with them, asked them questions that forced the shyest of them to open their mouths. One way or the other, good or bad, my mother ensured, compelled engagement.

One of my nephews, my youngest sister's eldest child, has an adopted daughter who was a year old when my mother fell ill and about five years old when she died, yet four years after my mother's passing, she was still asking,

"Uncle, where mama?" I was struck that she just couldn't forget my mother and took this as evidence of how strong an impression my mother, though bedridden, had made on her.

It was no different with adults. My mother would talk about gardening, herbal medicine, and seek to convert visitors to her Adventist faith. And she was always bearing gifts, be it Adventist pamphlets, advice solicited and unsolicited, the fruits of her garden, or the jams and condiments of her kitchen factory. Whatever fruit was in season, she would gather it daily to offer to visitors and send to neighbors, friends, and family.

It was impossible to leave my mother's presence with indifference. She was all-seeing, all-hearing. With her, there was no risk of not being seen. *I see you, I care about you, you are important, you are somebody.* In church, she noted all the children who were misbehaving, and one stare from her told them to straighten up right away.

My mother was people-centered. Her big-heartedness and engaging personality endeared her to people. Her life reflected the notion that it is people who are important; it is people who matter. As I'm entering old age and getting a better appreciation of the value of such engagement, I am grateful to have her example to follow.

A FEW YEARS BEFORE my mother fell ill, when one of her sisters living in the US called to inquire about her health, she would habitually tell her, "*Si sé pa kò, sé jip,*" meaning, if it isn't one thing, it's the other. So worried my mother wasn't doing too well, my aunt came down to spend time with her. About the fifth day of her visit, the sisters got into

Magna a memoir of the enduring human spirit

an altercation. It was never clear to me what brought it on. But it was such a violent quarrel—the obscene body language, the fierce facial expression, the intensity and harshness of the exchange—that I thought my aunt would depart that very day, and the sisters were unlikely to speak to each other for a long time.

But to my great surprise, within an hour of the confrontation, they made up and were laughing and talking like the fight had never occurred.

Afterward, in my mother's absence and by way of explanation, my aunt said that my mother was a bully. In her younger days, being timid, she allowed people like my mother to walk all over her, but in her mature age she insists on standing up for herself and telling bullies where to get off.

Notwithstanding, the episode was a revelation. It gave me an inkling of how fierce, combative, and competitive the sisters had been growing up in the twelve or sixteen-square-foot wooden house they called home. Yet it also revealed the strength of their familial bond, their sound emotional health, their emotional intelligence and agility.

If it were me, having engaged in such an exchange, I would be prepared never to talk with that person again for the rest of my life, or at least for a very long time. But wouldn't that have been immature, unproductive, a sign of emotional bankruptcy? One of human beings' greatest assets, greatest strengths, what helped them survive down through the ages, is the ability and willingness to cooperate, to work together to accomplish common goals and common tasks. But how can people work together if their rela-

How to Live a Healthy and Productive Life in Old Age

tionships can't return to normal after a heated disagreement or altercation?

Letting go and not taking things too much to heart was another of the lessons my mother's example taught me.

WHEN MY MOTHER FELL SICK, she suddenly became helpless and totally dependent, refusing to lift a finger on her own behalf, refusing to feed herself even if she could and even though the sickness had not diminished her appetite. She behaved with a great sense of entitlement, demanding what she wanted to eat and what she wanted us to do for her. When we didn't respond fast enough or refused to comply with those requests harmful to her, she would go straight into guilt-tripping us.

I thought, how could that be? Don't people say that you die the way you lived? That didn't seem to apply to my mother, a woman who had been so very independent and proactive, a woman I thought of as being in constant warfare. War against Vieux Fort to prevent the town from leading her children astray; war against her very own children, burning their books, imposing curfews, blocking them from mingling with "debauched" Vieux Fortians, taking the proverb "spare the rod, spoil the child" to a whole new level, all to safeguard their souls; war against the rocks and cliffs in her yard for coming in the way of her garden; war against the toads that made her garden their haven; war against starvation and destitution, hence her industriousness; war against hookworms and malnutrition that were robbing the health of her children; war against the school system to ensure her children get their fair share of education; war against diabetes, with exercise, diet, and medica-

Magna a memoir of the enduring human spirit

tion as ammunition; war to improve the quality of life of senior citizens and the otherwise poor and needy, as part of her church's Dorcas program. But now it seems my mother was perfectly happy to be totally dependent on others. As if she had laid down her weapons and was fighting war no more. I said, "Ah-ha, this must be a lesson on how not to die, how not to behave when you fall sick."

But then I started thinking, if you are already elderly and you fall sick and become bedridden, like it or not, you have no choice but to depend heavily on others. A caregiver has to devote a significant amount of her time, years of her life, even, taking care of you, which gives you plenty of time and reason to feel guilty about the sacrifice the person is making on your behalf, guilty that she is using up her life on old you. If you are thinking that way, how can you happily accept the help that your quality of life depends so much on? The only way to accept that help wholeheartedly, with no apologies, but maybe with some gratitude, is to reckon that you are more than entitled to it, that you are simply reaping the garden you lovingly and tenderly cultivated all those years, enjoying the fruits of your labor; or tapping into the savings account that you so patiently and diligently built up over so many years, withdrawing the accumulated interest. This way, you can maintain a healthy mindset about the help you are receiving, which your life depends on. Because if not, if you are riddled with guilt, don't you start wishing for an earlier demise so all this can pass?

So as my mother lay bedridden, she almost had me fooled that she had laid down her weapons and was fighting war no more. However, the only thing that had changed was the battlefield and the nature of the war. It was now a war

How to Live a Healthy and Productive Life in Old Age

against her death, a war against oblivion. With this new development, my mother had no choice but to change strategy, adopt new tactics, exchange her old weapons, useless in this new battlefield, for upgraded ones. Her entitled attitude was yet another lesson on how to maintain a healthy mental state while you lay dying, thus keeping the enemy called death at bay, prolonging your life as much as possible.

CHAPTER SIXTEEN

As My Mother Lay Dying

IN THE THIRD YEAR of my mother's bedridden illness, she had a mishap. She slipped and fell off the bed and fractured her hip. We were back at St. Jude Hospital. This time, she was kept for three weeks. By the time she was discharged, half of her buttocks had been taken over by bedsores, which would never completely heal and which, in the last few months of her life, grew worse. It took about three months at home to return to her pre-hip-injury routine of daily visits to the veranda.

In the latter half of 2020, the fourth year of my mother's bed confinement, her condition deteriorated rapidly. The bedsores got larger and deeper. Her feet became more swollen and got infected with bedsores. Her heart and lungs got weaker, and her blood circulation got poorer. She was sleeping more and more and was less and less lucid in her waking moments. Soon, we were forced to discontinue her trips to the veranda. Her vital systems were shutting down one by one. She was becoming all skin and bones. Yet she continued to soldier on, to hold on to life with every fiber, every cell in her body. Her appetite, her hunger, her zest for life seemingly as urgent as that of a newborn gasping for her first breath of air. Every so often, she would say to my sister, "Zel, *na mò,* Zel, I'm dying," but this only belied her hunger for life. I thought if not for this pneumonia, this bedridden-ness, my mother would have lived beyond a hundred years.

Soon, she could no longer chew and swallow food, so she had to be fed through a feeding tube. About this time, one of our neighbors, a retired nursing assistant and family friend, offered to help. She came two to three times daily, usually during feeding time and in the morning when my sister was giving my mother bed baths and treating her bed sores. So essentially the neighbor replaced me. I could see that her help and presence were a great relief to my sister beyond the actual physical service she provided. It came at a time when it was needed most, when my mother's health was rapidly going downhill, and probably when my sister's emotional resources were at their lowest. At this critical and taxing juncture, when the weight of my mother's life depended solely on her, my sister was gifted the assistance of a professional she trusted to carry some of the burden and share the responsibility of caring for my mother; someone whose help was unconditional and non-judgemental of her and the care she was providing. It was impossible to overstate the value of the neighbor's help to my sister.

My mother's situation had me thinking that life is so strange, so mysterious. There are people in their forties, fifties, and sixties who no sooner they fall sick, be it with cancer, stroke, or some other condition, quickly succumb to death, yet here was my ninety-one-year-old mother fighting so long, so hard, so desperately to hold on to life,

**Magna** a memoir of the enduring human spirit

to defeat death, underscoring the preciousness of life. Here she was, holding on nearly four years after recovering from a sickness that kills in the first month of infection about 30 percent of people her age. I couldn't help but wonder how some people, by their willingness, even eagerness to commit murder, could treat life as if it's nothing, could approach life with such callous disrespect. How could they place such a low value on this most precious of gifts?

As my mother lay dying, she imparted her final lesson to us. A lesson on valuing life, treating life as the greatest treasure, holding on to life up to our last breath. Again, I thought if not for the pneumonia, my mother would have lived way past a hundred years.

My mother held on so long to life that several of her family members who visited her at home or the hospital or who called from overseas to inquire about her health when it seemed she was the family member next in line to meet death died before her. So while my mother lay dying, her niece, Felicien Baptiste, died at 59 in St. Lucia in February 2017; her third oldest sibling and sister, Agnes Peters, died at 90 in Florida in September 2017; her sister, Josephine St. Hilaire, died at 81 in London in November 2017; and her nephew, Francis Peters, died at 54 in St. Lucia in January 2018.

My mother, who died around 3 AM on Sunday, December 20, 2020, at 91 years and 11 months, is so far the second longest-lived of the Francis clan. Only her oldest sibling, her sister Mary Francita St. Ange, who died in May 2023 at 97 years and 10 months, lived longer.

My mother's battle against death brought to mind the poet Dylan Thomas (1914-1953), for she certainly heeded

As My Mother Lay Dying

his admonishment and did not "go gentle into that good night." Instead, she raged "against the dying of the light."

I'm tempted to believe that my mother's refusal to go quietly and meekly into the night was her way of protecting her children. Somehow, she knew that we, her best things, would not have been able to cope with her death if she had died too hurriedly, too gently, so she took her time, raged against sleep for three years and eleven months, to allow us to adjust to her pending death, to enable us to grieve slowly, little by little, so by the time she passed we would have reconciled ourselves to the idea that she would die. In other words, by the time she died, we had done most of the grieving, and the grieving that remained to be done was within our power to handle. So even while my mother was dying, she was taking care of her children, her most precious.

My mother's Igbo cousins believed that when people who lived a just and societally responsible and dutiful life died, they became spirits called "living-dead" that occupied both the living and spirit worlds. Conversant in the language of gods as well as that of the living, these ancestral spirits serve as intermediaries between God and the living, and as such they protect their living descendants and visit and bless them with fertility, good health, and prosperity.

If we subscribe to this Igbo worldview that death is by no means the end of life but a mere transition from a physical to a spiritual realm that enables our ancestors to maintain connections with us from the afterlife, then we can rest assured that our mother is looking after us from the great beyond. After all, we, her children, were her most precious. And just as the ghost of her ancestors may have visited her while she lay dying, at some point in our lives we can expect

Magna a memoir of the enduring human spirit

her spirit to spend some time with us. I wonder what her ghost will be sharing with us.

My father died a different kind of death from my mother. He perished in a road accident at age 78 when he was still active and in good health. Until then he had been taking public transportation to town to pay his utility bills, and he was keeping bees and taking the occasional trip to his farm. He was still attending church and studying his daily Bible lessons. And he was still capable of enjoying his grandchildren and continuing to be a source of guidance, support and love to his children. His death short-circuited all of this, leaving us to contend with the shock and suddenness of it all, the rudeness of his departing with no time at all for us to prepare for his departure, to say goodbye, to receive his last words of admonishment, love and support. No time to get used to the notion that soon he would no longer be with us.

Of course, with my mother, the narrative was completely different. We had plenty of time to prepare—almost four years—to make amends or to seek resolution or absolution or revelation. But unlike my mother, my father was spared the loss of dignity, privacy, and independence, as well as the pain and suffering of a protracted, debilitating illness.

I asked myself, "Which is better? My father's sudden, premature exit or my mother's drawn-out passing? Better for whom? The children or the parents?" I'm glad the decision wasn't mine to make because I've yet to make up my mind.

Chapter Seventeen

Thou Shalt Surely Die

Throughout my mother's illness and after her death, I could not help but be troubled by how such a larger-than-life presence, such an indomitable spirit, such an always-on-your-feet persona could be reduced to such helplessness. How could those all-seeing eyes never again catch a glimpse of sunset, those all-hearing ears never again enjoy the morning symphony of crowing roosters, those never-lost-for-words lips never again curl around the names of her most precious?

My mother's illness and passing presented old age and death to me as a palpable, inescapable reality. The monition *Thou shalt surely die* took on much greater solidity. The mind is funny. It is one thing to think of something in the abstract, intellectually admit to its existence while avoiding the messiness, the emotion, the pain of coming to grips with its reality, but a totally different consideration when the truth of the abstraction is staring at you in its full starkness. If I were letting my mind play tricks on me, harboring doubts of the inevitability of my demise, thinking I was so special, so invincible, that old age, sickness and death might

Magna a memoir of the enduring human spirit

bypass me, my mother's departure burst that bubble, shattered that illusion, and clarified what was in store for me.

To watch the woman who could immobilize me with just a stare, who never lost an argument, never failed to find the right words to neutralize or demoralize an opponent, who was never wrong, could never be wrong, who was on her feet morning, noon and night, as if the physical limitations of time and biology didn't apply to her, reduced to such a state of helplessness that she couldn't feed herself, perform toiletry, even stand; that her body went decaying right in front of my eyes, her life-sustaining systems failing one by one, until she eventually lost her voice, orientation, her ability to eat, her grip on reality, is to know in no uncertain terms that death must come for me. If this indomitable woman, whom I had never imagined lying inert, whom I had never fully accepted wouldn't be around someday, exited this life in the most helpless, the most inauspicious manner, then how much more *thou shalt surely die* applies to me, a mere mortal. My mother's passing made my impending death as undeniable and as palpable as the salt-laden sea breeze that slaps me in the face when approaching Vieux Fort along its Atlantic coast.

The reality and inevitability of my mother's sickness and death had me wondering why all the greed, the selfishness, the big ego, the single-minded accumulation of wealth and power, if we are all, no matter how rich, how powerful, going to end up like my mother, helpless, stripped of all dignity, and eventually served up as meals for maggots.

As I watched my mother slowly, reluctantly, edging toward death, the person who once appeared to be indestructible, invincible, the person whose presence once filled the

Thou Shalt Surely Die

universe, I wondered what is the point of being born if we are all to end up dying. What is the point of things that don't last forever? Why go through all the trouble of being born and suffering growing pains and life's tribulations only to perish, to disappear? What is the purpose of all this? Indeed, what is the purpose of being born at all when this is what is in store for us?

I know my mother and her religion may answer: *we are here to serve God, and death is not the end, just a passage. The Kingdom of God awaits.* But this seems to be taking the easy way out. This appears to be a cop-out. My only solace, which wasn't much of a solace, was that this was the nature of things: the animals birth offspring that eventually replace them; the flowering trees bring forth fruits whose seeds scatter, germinate, and become the trees that keep the forest alive; the banana plants sprout offshoots, suckers they are called, that replace the parents after they have borne fruit, wither and die. We are not exempt from nature's cycle. Without death, life is much less interesting, much less exciting, much less precious, much less urgent. Without death, there would be much less variety, and fewer people would have walked the earth. Without death, some of us probably would never have been born. We exist because those in the past have died. Without death, there is no life. So the desire to live forever, though natural—notice how fiercely creatures of all kinds fight for survival— is selfish; it's nothing but greed and arrogance.

In lashing out, I said to myself, we see the animals and plants die and decay, yet we never ask why they had to die. But we think we are so significant that we can't accept our death for what it is, so we invent a utopian afterlife, which we never envisioned for plants and animals. We want to live forever. Well, nature has designed a better way for us to live forever, meaning beyond our own lives. Nature has made self-perpetuation in terms of biology or genetics the ultimate purpose of life, the instrument by which we live forever.

In terms of culture, the example of our parents' lives teaches us how best to live a life and thus be better able to pass on our culture to the next generation. However, there can be a conflict between the perpetuation of culture and biology. Having many children is a plus for perpetuating our biology, but with many children we are less able to do a credible job of passing on our culture to each child.

Notwithstanding, my mother was one of the lucky ones. She lived to the ripe old age of one month shy of ninety-two, and right up to her eighty-seventh birthday, she lived a relatively active, productive, and independent life. And during her illness, she had her nine children, her most precious, doting over her, some regularly crossing oceans to spend time with her. Moreover, she had her very own private nurse, her eldest daughter and best friend, administering loving, tender, and dedicated care. So much so that I don't think it's possible to give anyone better care than my sister gave my mother.

Despite all this musing, long after my mother was gone, now and again, the disconcerting thought that she was gone for good and the incredulity of it all would pierce my consciousness.

I lost my mother the first time at the tender age of between 12 and 15 months when she departed for London, and I lost her a second time at the mature age of 62 when she departed for the grave. I suspect the first loss was the most painful, the most debilitating, but I also suspect the second loss fed from the agony of the first.

In *The Last Rose of Shanghai*, a novel by Weina Dai Randel, the protagonist said, "A family without a mother, was like a pearl necklace without a string." I agree wholeheartedly. My mother was the one keeping the family's pearl necklace intact; she was the string, and with her gone the necklace is shattered, the pearls scattered. When my father died, I wondered what evil he was holding at bay that now he is gone will be unleashed on the family. Yet in his absence, the family held together, a strong sense of family remained. Now, with my mother gone, I feel we have become less of a family; her children living overseas have much less reason to visit their homeland. Without my mother, without the string, I'm afraid the pearls, my mother's most precious, that once formed the necklace will be permanently dispersed.

CHAPTER EIGHTEEN

A Lesson on How Best to Die

WATCHING MY SISTER dedicating her life to caring for my mother, willingly sacrificing her well-being for that of my mother, and knowing that providing such care takes a toll on caregivers, even to the extent of shortening their lives, I couldn't help but question the fairness of burdening someone else, preventing them from living their own life when one has already lived a full and ripened life. Why trade the life of a still productive 67-year-old, with possibly fifteen-plus years of good quality life remaining, for an incapacitated 90-year-old who has apparently reached the end of her productive life and who at best has just a few more years left? I had the distinct impression that if it were at all possible, my sister would gladly have given up her life for my mom to live on, the way parents would do for their children.

As my mother lay dying, she taught me yet another lesson, or rather she brought me to the new realization that, notwithstanding what I said about the value of holding on to life with all one's might for as long as possible, I don't

A Lesson on How Best to Die

want to live past the point where I become incapable of taking care of my basic physical needs. I don't wish someone to sacrifice their life for me when I've already lived mine. I don't want to go in the manner of my father, but neither do I wish to depart like my mother. Somewhere in between would be my preference. My mother taught me how to live, and she clarified for me how I wish to die.

Why spend so many resources on the soon-to-be departed while so many children, their whole life ahead of them, are dying or subjected to stunted development out of poverty, starvation, lack of medical care, and unsanitary living conditions? My mother's circumstances forced me to dwell on these uncomfortable, disconcerting realities. My sister's dedication brought to mind the Asian culture of ancestor worship. In fact, on one extreme, we have some cultures, for example, the southern Indian state of Tamil Nadu, that practice senicide. On the other end, we have the common Asian culture of venerating the elderly to the point of worshiping their ancestors as gods.

Of course, we—my mother's children—had no choice. We were acculturated to take care of our parents in their old age. This was the contract we signed at birth. Our parents made enormous sacrifices for us as children, and as adults we pay back by taking care of them in their declining years. Consciously or unconsciously, intentionally or not, our parents made sure we were aware of the contract. During our growing up, they would discuss people who didn't take care of their parents in their old age, and based on how our parents discussed this unfortunate turn of events, the emotion and disgust in their voices, and the curse they said would befall the perpetrators, and how the children who took care of their parents were blessed, I had the distinct impression that neglecting one's parents was one of the most disgusting crimes someone could commit. Each time these conversations came up, I silently pledged to make sure I took care of my parents in their old age. And I suspect the same was true for all my siblings.

Indeed, in traditional agrarian societies, where self-employment is the order of the day, there are no pensions, health insurance plans, or social safety nets. So besides serving as a source of unpaid labor, the children were the parents' medical insurance and social security plans. Of course, in my generation, my siblings have fewer children: two have three, one has two, and the rest have one or none. Besides, with their savings, job pensions, and health insurance, they can financially care for themselves in their old age. There is also the compulsion of parents to leave property behind for their children. My parents could have sold their lands and used the money as cushion in their old age, but that would have violated the contract of bequeathing their children assets.

Notwithstanding all this rumination, I must hasten to say that this was just the intellect talking, and, as the saying goes, talk is cheap. It is one thing to engage in rational thought, but a whole different thing when primal, gut feelings and reactions take hold. Every time we had to call the ambulance to take my mother to the hospital, shock waves would pass through my head, and I would grow weak and have difficulty speaking. At such times, what overwhelmed me, incapacitated me, was the thought that my mother was dying, and I knew that guilt or no guilt, productivity or not, usefulness or not, I would do anything to prevent this from

A Lesson on How Best to Die

happening. I wasn't sure I could or would survive my mother's death. Her dying was my dying. Economics, fairness, wastage, morality, were the furthest things from my mind. *My mother was dying, but my mother cannot not die,* would dominate, overwhelm my existence.

MY MOTHER IS GONE, but I take some solace in that having passed on her genetic material to us, she has defeated death and ensured her immortality. But genetics isn't the only thing she has passed on to us, and it isn't the only way she has defeated death. She has passed on her accumulated knowledge of how best to live a life, and she lives on in our memories. This is probably what has led Igbos and many other African societies to the belief that death is not about the ending of life but about a natural transition from a physical to a spiritual existence that enables ancestors to maintain connections with their descendants in the afterlife.

If culture is the manifestation of the way of life of a people and women are bearers of their people's culture, my mother has passed on a culture to her children by the example of her life, by the lessons she taught and exemplified on how best to live a life.

My mother was indeed a great woman; she was the stuff legends are made of. I thank her for her indomitable spirit. No matter her shortcomings, we, her children, her most precious, are blessed for having been raised and nurtured under her wings. Her church and community have been enriched by having fellowshipped with her. Though she is gone, she will forever remain in our hearts. May her exploits and heroics, which she never failed to narrate, echo through the ages. Though she is gone in the physical, I will hold on to the beliefs of my Igbo ancestors that her spirit will be communing with us from the afterlife.

CHAPTER NINETEEN

The Eulogy

MY BROTHER, the college professor, gave the Eulogy at my father's funeral and, two decades later, honored us again with the eulogy at my mother's funeral. His eulogy for our father was included in the memoir *My Father Is No Longer There.* So perhaps, if nothing else but for symmetry and balance, it is fitting to end this memoir with his eulogy for my mother.

Brothers and Sisters, Friends and Family, Ladies and Gentlemen. Our mother was a spirited and compassionate lady whose life was animated by her unwavering and passionate commitment to nurturing her immediate and extended family, serving her God and church, and caring for the sick, the poor, and the dispossessed in her community. To those of you who have chosen to join us in person despite the obvious perils of the ongoing pandemic and to those of you in the diaspora and in St. Lucia who have joined us via social media, I say thank you. Thank you very much for choosing to bear witness to our acknowledgement that after completing her life's work with distinction, Mama has made a graceful exit.

Magna a memoir of the enduring human spirit

Just under nineteen years ago, at the behest of my siblings, I stood at this very podium to eulogize our father—St. Brice Reynolds (aka Bro Si). At the time, I considered it a privilege and high honor, and I still do. Today, I am again deeply honored and humbled by the opportunity to eulogize our mother—Philomene "Francis" Reynolds. In reviewing the eulogy I wrote for our father, I was drawn to my summation of his role in the creation and evolution of this family. That summation read as follows.

> *. . . with the desire to be like Jesus as his guide, with our mother as his partner, and with the Almighty's benevolence, this family and its legacy were built day by day, son by son, daughter by daughter, and lesson by lesson.*

This reference to our mother as Bro Si's partner requires elaboration, and it is fitting that I do so today. In an age of machismo, our mother was an equal partner in the Reynolds family enterprise; she was a font of creativity when bold imagination was required and an entrepreneur who amplified seemingly insufficient resources into enough to feed, clothe, and educate her nine children plus nurture many others in our extended family and community.

Our mother was a formidable lady. She was endowed with the confidence, the will, and strength of character that made her a veritable force of nature. Like forces of nature, she did not succumb to obstacles to achieving the many worthy objectives she pursued over

The Eulogy

a lifetime of achievement in her roles as daughter, sister, wife, mother, and leader in her church (this church).

It is sometimes possible to discover a person's defining attributes by observing their pursuit of a particular activity, vocation, or avocation. Mama was a life-long gardener. When physical limitations made it impossible for her to garden, she did it anyway: by issuing instructions from her wheelchair or bed. During a forlorn walk around Mama's yard on the day after I was released from quarantine, it dawned upon me that Mama's gardening was the avocation that was most likely to reveal her defining attributes.

It might be argued that there are three essential steps in gardening. These are tilling or preparation of the soil, planting, and nurturing (fertilizing, weeding, pruning, etc.). Ma Sido's success as a gardener would not have been possible without her flawless execution of these indispensable steps. With your indulgence, I will now recount a few anecdotes that I hope will demonstrate who she was.

When Ma Sido determined that an expansion of her kitchen garden was necessary, the fact that she had already cultivated every bit of arable land in the yard into an already impressive kitchen garden did not in any way dampen her enthusiasm for the project. In fact, she proceeded to transform the rocky hillside immediately above our house on New Dock Lane into arable land. How, you might ask? Well, when soil was excavated for an extension of the house, she enlisted every one of us in a bucket-by-bucket transfer of the excavated soil up to the rocky hillside. When soil was excavated for a septic tank she did it again. To enhance the fertility of the topsoil she required us to make regular trips to the mangue to collect dried cow dung (known in these parts as *kaka bèf*). Before long, she was harvesting peas, green peppers, and sweet potatoes from the formerly rocky hillside. When the family moved to our house on St. Jude's Highway, Mama again cultivated every bit of land in the yard. When she ran out of land, she started erecting elevated boxes and even produced yams in the carcass of an old refrigerator. *You see, one of Mama's defining attributes is that she understood that success in any endeavor required preparation. Another defining attribute is that she did not easily succumb to obstacles. She assessed them, found ways around them, and frequently converted them into opportunities. These attributes influenced her performance in every role she undertook and every endeavor she pursued.*

Planting is an act of investing. You plant the seed. You devote resources to its development and growth. You exercise the discipline and patience to wait for the results. Mama planted many, many seeds during the course of her life. Some became plants that grew to produce fruits and vegetables. Some were seeds of hope and opportunity that made it possible for a dispossessed child to thrive into a productive adult. Others were seeds of kindness that told those who felt invisible that she saw them and that they were worthy. Most of all she planted seeds that produced discipline, industriousness, compassion, and self-belief in her children. *Mama was a planter of seeds.*

The Eulogy

After seeds are planted, they must be *nurtured*. You must water them when there is no rain, fertilize when appropriate, remove the weeds that inevitably threaten to suffocate them, and prune when necessary. Mama did all those things in her garden, but most importantly she excelled in doing them in every facet of her life. Take weeding for example. Weeds in a garden are like associating with the wrong crowd. Mama limited our exposure to unsavory influencers by weeding them out of our lives.

In her roles as daughter, sister, wife, mother, and Dorcas leader, *Mama was a preparer; Mama was a planter; Mama was a nurturer. Therefore, Mama was a gardener.*

It is impossible to write a credible characterization of our mother's life without recognizing the special relationship she enjoyed with my sister Ezildra Poleon (better known as Zel). Highlighting this special relationship is not intended in any way to diminish Ma Sido's love and regard for her other kids and we (Zel's siblings) do not resent it. Instead, it is a relationship that we venerate; that is Shakespearean in its intensity, complexity, and durability; and that is the most profound illustration of filial love and devotion of which I am aware.

An individual's commitment or devotion to a person, family, or organization can be measured by looking at what they are willing to give up to serve that person, family, or organization. By that standard, Zel's commitment to our mother and this family is both infinite and unfathomable. There is no burden she did not bear; there is no price she deemed too high, and there was no slight she did not forgive. As our mother approached the end of her sojourn and her suffering intensified, Zel never flinched from being present and suffered along with her without complaint. Zel, your life of service, sacrifice, and selflessness locates you in the company of the saintly and the angelic. They say that there is a great woman behind every great man. Today, I say that there is a supportive and enduring husband enabling Zel's extraordinary commitment to our mother and family. For this, Bro Stan, we thank you.

Great gardeners deserve to reap a bountiful harvest. God blessed Mama with longevity that allowed her to see the results of the many seeds she planted. It is my fervent hope and belief that at the moment of her passing, having cleared a glide path to the pearly gates, God's angels carried her on their wings to meet the Almighty who welcomed her with open arms and gave our departed gardener a tour of the Garden of Eden. Thank you. Thank you very much!

Author Note

Thanks plenty for reading *Magna* I hope you found it a worthwhile read. I'm very much interested in what you thought of it, and I'm sure other readers would, too, so it would mean a lot to me for you to leave a review on Amazon, Goodreads, or other online platforms.

Also, please visit my author page (via QR code) to follow me on my writing journey, explore my other books, and join our email list to receive our newsletter, blogs, and news of book releases, tours, exclusive content, giveaways, and other activities.

Glossary

Abizan abusive

Anba bwa in the woods

Abondans free spending

Bef mové mad cow

Béja a form of rotating savings club

Carrier aluminum food container with two or three compartment levels

Esusu traditional Yoruba and Igbo rotating savings club akin to the St. Lucia susu

Fanmchay midwife

Font valley, bottom

Gadè seer, obeah man/woman, a practitioner of obeah

Gens libres free people of color

Gwan bwa forest, dense woodland

Gwenn anba fèy a medicinal herb

Jan gajé person who do others harm or mischief with witchcraft

Jouné pwété literally loaned day, a form of communal labor that involves trading labor

kabann bedding of sacs and rags

Kannòt vwèl canoe or pirogue with sails

Glossary

Kay pay straw hut with dirt floors

Kolonm plantation overseers

Kont stories or songs (usually about the deceased) performed at wakes

Koton nwè black cotton cloth

Koudmen a help, a free work day (cooperative self-help)

Kutumba an African-derived dance in which drumming plays a prominent role in the music

Ladjablès bewitching female spirits known to cause people to get lost

Layette money set aside to purchase the needs of a new born

Lok purge given after childbirth

Lonbwi navel, umbilical cord

Maho Piman a tree whose bark can be stripped to make rope; the name also refers to the rope made from such a tree.

Makabou a banana variety with short thick fruit/vegetable

Maman de l'eau mermaid who lured men into deep water to drown them

méchansté wicked, evil, abusive

Glossary

Neg maron originally, meant fugitive or escaped slaves

Papicho nonsense, foolishness

Pòdjab poor devil, poor thing, pitiful

Sevyé boards on which a coffin is carried, normally by four men

Si sé pa kò, sé jip if it isn't bodice, it is skirt; meaning, it is always one thing or the other

Siyé bwa log sawing

Susu a form of rotating savings group

Tann èk konpwann hear and understand

Tizan a tea given to women after giving birth

Ti bolom supernatural being in the form of a toddler with oversized head

Tou san fon bottom-less pit

Woulé la ba a form of cricket in which the ball is pitched underhand

Notes/References

1. Reynolds, A. (2021). *No Man's Land: A Political Introspection of St. Lucia.* (pp. 200-202). Vieux Fort St. Lucia: Jako Books.

2. Loop St. Lucia News. *(2018, October 23). VF4Cs call for action on St. Jude Hospital.* Retrieved from https://stlucia.loopnews.com/content/vf4cs-call-action-st-jude-hospital

3. Mintz, S. *Historical Context: Facts about the Slave Trade and Slavery.* The Glider Lehrman Institute of American History. Retrieved from https://www.gilderlehrman.org/history-resources/teacher-resources/historical-context-facts-about-slave-trade-and-slavery

4. Devaux, Robert J. (1997). *They Called Us Brigands: The Saga of St. Lucia's Freedom Fighters.* (pp. 69, 72). Castries, St. Lucia: Robert J Devaux.

5. Gladman J, Barer D, Venkatesan P, Berman P, Macfarlane J. (1991). *The outcome of pneumonia in the elderly: a hospital survey. Clinical Rehabilitation,* 5(3):201-205. doi:10.1177/026921559100500305

6. VERENNA, K. S. (2022). Elderly Pneumonia Survival Rate. *Griswold.* Retrieved from https://www.griswoldhomecare.com/blog/2022/july/elderly-pneumonia-survival-rate/

Notes/References

7. Harmsen, J., Ellis, G., and Devaux, R. (2012). *A History of St. Lucia* (pp. 119-120). Cape Moule A Chique, Vieux Fort, St. Lucia: Light House Road Publications.

8. Ellie Shearer, E. (2019). *Memories Of Caribbean Slavery: Past Injustice, Present Subjectivity, and the Possibility of Repair.* MPhil Thesis, University of Oxford.

9. Lawrence, M. B., Pelissier, J. M. (1981). Atlantic Hurricane Season of 1980. *Monthly Weather Review*, Vol. 109, pp. 1567-1582. Retrieved from https://www.aoml.noaa.gov/hrd/hurdat/mwr_pdf/1980.pdf

10. Reynolds, A. (2003). *The Struggle for Survival: An historical, political, and socioeconomic perspective of St. Lucia* (Third Edition, pp. 87-103, 170-205). Vieux Fort St. Lucia: Jako Books.

11. Reynolds, A. (2023). *They Called Him Brother George: Portrait of a Caribbean Politician.* (pp. 8-36). Vieux Fort St. Lucia: Jako Books.

12. Peter, Laurence. (2019, October 24). Pesticide poisoned French paradise islands in Caribbean. *BBC News.* Retrieved from https://www.bbc.com/news/world-europe-50144261

13. Royal Museums Greenwich. *The story of the Windrush.* Retrieved from https://www.rmg.co.uk/stories/windrush-histories/story-of-windrush-ship

Notes/References

14. Theravive. (2024). *Reactive Attachment Disorder DSM-5 313.89 (F94.1.* Retrieved from https://www.theravive.com/therapedia/reactive-attachment-disorder-dsm—5-313.89-(f94.1)

15. Ellis, E.E., Yilanli, M., and Saadabadi, A. (2023). *Reactive Attachment Disorder.* National Library of Medicine. Retrieved from https://www.ncbi.nlm.nih.gov/books/NBK537155/

16. Wan, W. (2018, June 18). What separation from parents *does to children: The effect is catastrophic. The Washington Post.* Retrieved from https://www.washingtonpost.com/national/health-science/what-separation-from-parents-does-to-children-the-effect-is-catastrophic/2018/06/18/c00c30ec-732c-11e8-805c-4b67019fcfe4_story.html

17. Harmsen, J. (2019). *A Review of My Father Is No Longer There.* Retrieved from https://www.jakoproductions.com/my-father-is-no-longer-there-by-anderson-reynolds/

18. Halloran, M. J. (2019). African American Health and Posttraumatic Slave Syndrome: A Terror Management Theory Account. *Journal of Black Studies,* 50(1), 45-65. https://doi.org/10.1177/0021934718803737

Notes/References

19. Jiang S, Postovit L, Cattaneo A, Binder EB, Aitchison KJ. (2019, November 8). Epigenetic Modifications in Stress Response Genes Associated With Childhood Trauma. *Front Psychiatry.* 2019 Nov 8;10:808. doi: 10.3389/fpsyt.2019.00808. PMID: 31780969; PMCID: PMC6857662.

20. Ekmekci, H.S., Muftareviç, S. (2023). Epigenetic Effects of Social Stress and Epigenetic Inheritance. *Current Approaches in Psychiatry* 2023; 15(1):132-145. https://dergipark.org.tr/en/download/article-file/2198008

21 Connie J. Mulligan, C.J. (2016). Early Environments, Stress, and the Epigenetics of Human Health. *ANNUAL REVIEW OF ANTHROPOLOGY,* Vol. 45:233-249. https://doi.org/10.1146/annurev-anthro-102215-095954

22. Morrison, T. (2019, August 6). *White People Have a Very Very Serious Problem—*Toni Morrison on Charlie Rose. Retrieved from https://youtu.be/n2txzMkT5Pc

23. Sloman, S. and Fernbach, P. (2017). *The Knowledge Illusion: Why we never think alone.* New York, New York: Riverhead Books.

24. Fraser, G.E., and Shavlik, D.J. (2001). *Ten Years of Life: Is It a Matter of Choice?* Arch Intern Med. 161(13), 1645–1652. doi:10.1001/archinte.161.13.1645

THE WORLD OF ANDERSON REYNOLDS

They Called Him Brother George: Portrait of a Caribbean Politician "A very engaging and excellent summary of our political history ... a wonderful reconstruction of George Odlum's life from the people who knew him best." —**Samuel Bowers, author of *Talking Truth to St. Lucian Power***

No Mans Land: A Political Introspection of St. Lucia "A no-holds-barred analysis of St. Lucia's current political environment. This timely dissection of the anatomy of St. Lucia's body politic is certain to ruffle a few feathers. Awesome... profound, informative, and thought-provoking." —**Dr. James Fletcher, Former Cabinet Minister**

My Father Is No Longer There "A biography and an autobiography, as well as an important addition to our understanding of the unwitting impact of West Indian migration on the psyche of the children involved. A love ballad, a joy to read, a privilege to be savoured."— **Dr. Jolien Harmsen, author of *A History of St. Lucia.***

The Stall Keeper "an excellent writer, his characters and situation literally jump off the page,...provides a fascinating and relatable glimpse into a culture that's little known and mysterious to most Americans."—**Writer's Digest** "Arguably the best novel to come out of St. Lucia." —**Mc Donald Dixon, author of *A Scream in the Shadows***

The Struggle for Survival: an historical, political, and socioeconomic perspective of St. Lucia "An impressive piece of narration...A veritable tapestry of St. Lucian life and culture ... Easily one of the most compelling pieces of literature I have laid hands on in recent years." —**Modeste Downes, author of *Phases***

Death by Fire "... an invaluable book... In a very definite way, establishes the St. Lucian personality, the St. Lucian national and cultural identity." —**Jacques Compton, Author of *a troubled dream*** "A novel on a grand scale...a key to the feeling and conscience of the age in which we live." —**The Crusader**

About the Author

ANDERSON REYNOLDS was born and raised in Vieux Fort, St. Lucia, where he resides. He holds a PhD in Food and Resource Economics from the University of Florida. Besides *Magna*, he is the author of six national bestselling books, namely the memoir *My Father Is No Longer There*, the award-winning novels *Death by Fire* and *The Stall Keeper*, the award-winning creative nonfiction *The Struggle For Survival: an historical, political, and socioeconomic perspective of St. Lucia*, the political biography *They Called Him Brother George: Portrait of a Caribbean Politician*, and the political treatise *No Man's Land: A Political Introspection of St. Lucia*. His books, blogs, lectures, and newspaper and magazine articles have established him as one of his country's leading public intellectuals and a foremost authority on its socioeconomic history.